The Multi-Level Perspectives of Agribusiness

The Multi-Level Perspectives of Agribusiness

Amedzro St-Hilaire, Walter
University of Ottawa, Canada

World Scientific

NEW JERSEY • LONDON • SINGAPORE • BEIJING • SHANGHAI • HONG KONG • TAIPEI • CHENNAI • TOKYO

Published by

World Scientific Publishing Co. Pte. Ltd.
5 Toh Tuck Link, Singapore 596224
USA office: 27 Warren Street, Suite 401-402, Hackensack, NJ 07601
UK office: 57 Shelton Street, Covent Garden, London WC2H 9HE

British Library Cataloguing-in-Publication Data
A catalogue record for this book is available from the British Library.

THE MULTI-LEVEL PERSPECTIVES OF AGRIBUSINESS

ISBN 978-981-3271-07-4

For any available supplementary material, please visit
http://www.worldscientific.com/worldscibooks/10.1142/11008#t=suppl

Desk Editor: Sandhya Venkatesh

Typeset by Stallion Press
Email: enquiries@stallionpress.com

Printed in Singapore

To Yemina,
Thank you for existing!

"The class is the opulence of the great innovative ideas to shake the prerequisites."

Dr. Amedzro St-Hilaire, Walter

TABLE OF CONTENTS

INTRODUCTION

Confronted with mutations of unprecedented diversity and intensity during the last decades, the production sector in agribusiness has been able to achieve a true silent revolution, and resolutely embrace modernity. Far from closing on itself, it has been able to challenge itself, leverage its many assets, and open to many new problematics to cover many multiple dimensions today.

The first one certainly lies in close relationship between the sector, its natural environment, and the rural area where it is spread. Indeed, what would be a world without an agroforestry sector? Obviously, not so much, especially if we consider the important part it has in the overall area, whose physiognomy is depicted as being both regular and varied. The human factor is also essential: forestry is the main activity of millions of people who live from it daily. Contributing, prominently in valorizing the landscape while providing raw materials to many industries, the wooded areas represent, today, in the world, a key point of the agroforestry problematic.

This harmonious combination has a major role not only in protecting the environment, maintaining the fauna and flora biodiversity, but also in fighting against global warming by storing carbon. Moreover, it offers an exceptional natural setting that is essential to preserve by developing environment-friendly means of production, said to be "qualified."

The human aspect is also an essential dimension we can qualify as original from a historical point of view of the sector. It made of this sector a worldwide exporter of processed agroforestry products and raw agroforestry products. This great success put the dynamism of workers on the fact that the opportunity of national and community support strategies generates an extremely diverse production: the world benefits from this diverse production whose quality and local connection has been conserved (fortunately). Thus, and it has to be remembered, the global agroforestry sector has, a genetic wood heritage of exceptional value.

The establishment of a special system acknowledging and protecting the origin and the quality of production has indeed permitted to join to the "brand," a particular aura that the sector can only benefit from exporting. Meanwhile, the development of a true "traceability" in a context of increased international trades and recurrence of health crisis, would, without a doubt, add a value to their production. These evolutions, which affected the entire global agroforestry sector during the last decades, have been followed, through the rationalization of materials and techniques, by the reduction of costs, that workers directly benefited from: the part of agroforestry in the total budget thus went from 50 percent to 11 percent in fifty years.

A sector of quality whose productions, accessible to others, are not only safe but also beneficial to the environment, it seems to be the third characteristic to consider from now. On one hand, the establishment of a highly sophisticated system of security control, despite the frequent crisis, guaranteed the perfect safety of the products of this sector throughout the world. On the other hand, the growing awareness of the concerned actors (public power, producers, consumers) of consequences on the environment, led to privilege favorable factors for the preservation of the environment.

The last unavoidable aspect of the future: energy and, globally, the biomass valuation. Almost completely ignored about ten years ago, these aspects have steadily developed to the point of being now one of the most important challenges of the future. The sector has been a provider of sustainable energy from an environmental point of view, able to reduce the global energy dependence while promoting rural areas: the millions of tons of biofuels produced are only the beginning of a larger development plan of biofuels leading to their incorporation at a rate of 10 percent in the near future. However, let there be no mistake: regarding the necessarily limited nature of areas, their mobilization in favor of biofuels will only be partial and temporary.

Beyond the few crops, it is the entire biomass that is mobilized today, and the forest first, the million cubic meters of wood used each year already cover 7 percent of the global energy needs. But energy is not the only way to promote products of this sector, far from it: solvents, lubricants, surfactants, building materials, packaging, cosmetics, plastics ... can now be made on economic and environmental terms with forest resources.

The sector is now confronted with the challenge of sustainability in the three different aspects of the concept. First of all, the primary sector has to ensure its productive function, historically first, under satisfactory conditions of competitiveness and at a sufficiently large scale to meet the needs of the entire demand. Then, this activity of production has to be part of a protected environment and responsibly manage natural resources. Finally, it must consider the human dimension, in its social component as well.

A competitive and qualitative production, respectful of man and nature, which is the future challenge this sector will have to meet. This book is aimed at highlighting the conditions of this sustainability as well as the conditions of adaptation of mechanisms related to agribusiness. One of the major challenges of this book was to take a look beyond the "upstream" to reach a "panoramic" view of the general context in which agroforestry strategies meet the global agro-production.

A quick observation reveals that the sector is a major asset in the world. However its sustainability was threatened by internal as well as external pressures. In this difficult context, the "conquest of added value," going through a combination of factors between the different phases of the products valuation (production, processing, or distribution), in a vertical logic, that is, sector by sector, seemed to be an interesting track, considering that the production complex has considerably evolved over the last century, gradually giving up the idea of a self-centered traditional sector to open up to new forms and development structures.

It now gathers millions of people in extremely diverse fields all over the world, from production to distribution, through supply and transformation. Marked by a common tertiary phenomenon in the entire global economy, even if the manual option remains relevant, it successively went from the artisanal stage to an industrial one, and finally tertiary, where research of growth and added value focuses more and more on immaterial elements. A systemic approach emphasizes the existence, in the global agroforestry system, of so-called "operating" subsystems — subsystems of "information," and subsystem of "decision" — all three interacting globally.

This global system is subjected to different types of forces, and first to natural forces. The recent demographic projections showed that earth will have around ten billion of people in the next years, a ceiling that will be followed by a stabilization phase. This demographic transition partly governs the qualitative and quantitative evolution of global needs. Applied to the only population of this sector, the demographic projections reveal a reduction in agroforestry, raising the question of farm transfers and of young farmer's settlement. To these demographic pressures are added the climatic and environmental forces.

The recent global awareness, of the "finite" and fragile nature of the biosphere, as well as the risk related to accelerate global warming of earth due to the excessive release of greenhouse gases, has directly been reflected on sectorial challenges: the management of predictable water shortage, modification in terms of its geography, the establishment of production techniques respecting the environment, the consideration of "carbon footprint," the development of the "biofuel" field.

To the natural conflicts are added those by humans and the institutions they create, in order to manage production and exchanges. The productivity differentials between the "wealthy" and "poor" regions exclude the total liberalization of trade: more than increasing the inequity of development, already substantial, its side effects will be to intensify market volatility and question the state sovereignty of many producing countries. Besides, such liberalization, that certainly benefit certain agents, is not necessarily beneficial globally. In contrast, strategies relating to subassemblies to similar economic characteristic must be developed. Thinking about the production sector today implies diversity, which also means "wood."

The projections disclose scenarios of development for each region characterized by its choices of specialization, the public service level of intervention, and the level of the openness to trade. The world should witness a return to a relatively emphasized specialization of regions. Simulations determine four different scenarios fostering respectively the rural, industrial, identity, and tertiary aspect of such development. If the recent legislative evolutions present notable improvement throughout the world, they keep away from choosing between many scenarios and do not offer a specific project from the rural areas.

This one now remains marked with the cooperative model able to organize production for each of its member, but also to participate in other fields in order to expand its activity to the entire agroforestry perimeter, especially downstream. In a symmetrical movement, the major industries of production seek to ensure a direct relationship between producers to secure supply. The system is marked by an increasing interpenetration of operators and activities, the production representing only one step between others. If an industrial field is still recognizable; it is, however, defined by its considerable heterogeneity, including very numerous small- and medium-sized companies employing an important part of staff, but also some large companies realizing most of the sector turnover. If the latter remains the most important of the industry, it is still marked by a degradation of the growth and the margins, as well as the loss of competitiveness and market shares for the benefit of the agro-production.

The way of salvation seems to go through an increase of research and development spending in order to respond to the growth of consumers' needs, as well as a more offensive strategy in fast-growing market. The most dynamic markets are those privileging internationalization, innovation, and the research of complimentary activities. For these groups, investment fund represents valuable instruments of financing whose requirements in terms of profitability induce the business leaders to adopt a strategic position in sectors with a high growth potential of ... it is now required to step in, to direct the evolution of the forest system, in each of its component. The use of an excellent organism of research must be optimized: for instance, it should be given to production-environment studies, the means to function and value the results of their researches.

Maintaining their productivity, the practices must continue to evolve to contribute to an increasing respect of the environment and biodiversity. The major producing regions must adapt their structures and development strategies to the predictable modifications of the sector to stay in line with the demand. Everywhere, they have to globalize to favor the setting up, on certain territories, of industries, in search of tightened links with the suppliers of raw products. In rural areas, poles of competitiveness, quality of life, lived up by a tight network of small- and medium-sized companies, must be set up to drain the income of the current: residents and tourists.

At the institutional level, in particular, the necessity of preserving real sectorial strategies must be reaffirmed by putting forward the fact that mechanisms have to be conceived to regulate the volatility of markets and remunerate exactly the positive amenities brought by the sector to the entire society. As the production will still exist, its profile will evolve considerably: there will be less competent operators managing recomposed structures, natural and logistic disparities will tend to become more radical, an industry, which added value keep concentrating in a reduced number of actors, a greater importance of export in the context of a saturated market; a neglect of the price factor in the act of purchase in the profit of ecological, sanitary or ethical elements, symbols of an increased attention to individual and its place in the biosphere.

In such a context, certain events and justifiable questions increase big fears against the agro-production. Does this mean that the agribusiness system is on the wrong track? Unknown for years, unrecognized for decades, for a long time considered aside, not comparable to the industrial world; today, agribusiness is at its cross-road. If it succeeded in its Fordism transformation and is now the first global industrial sector in terms of turnover, while generating a very significant trade balance, nevertheless, it seems very fragile. Having a little gone away, and not without consequences, from the agricultural upstream, while transforming globally a significant part of the production, agribusiness is indeed in the eye of the cyclone: pointed for its tendency to concentration, both by producers and consumers, considered by others as a little respectful of social and environmental standards, the global agro-production is now confronted with the challenges of durability.

This interrogation may seem a little reducing of the sector of agro-production. However, it is the one that each one of us settles: the farmer, who more than ever, must know how much and to whom to sell before producing; the employee who needs a successful and respectful work environment; the distributor who has to look for the product asked by the consumer who desires today a healthy, safe, and cheap product. The public decision maker, who, to govern has to plan.

The concern to center the reflection on this key question led deliberately the author to abstain from presenting an exhaustive picture of agro-production. Furthermore, the statistic definition of the notion of agro-production turns out to be difficult. This one gathers, indeed, the processing activities of agricultural and food products and excludes wholesale and detail trade of these products. The sharing between neither is still obvious, nor constant. Therefore, for a long time, bakery is ranked in the agro-production industries, while the butchery belongs to retail trade. On the other hand, the slaughter of cattle, hardly distinguished from the butchery, was classified sometimes in the wholesale trade, sometimes in the agro-production. The book, wanted to show how, in several years; this business sector had been able to achieve an unprecedented transformation. If such an assertion cannot be enough for the consumer, for the entrepreneur, or for the decision maker in its reflection on the future, it allows nevertheless to observe and to consider this sector with a minimum of objectivity. When the agribusiness models are dragged into the mud, and when we wonder about their medium-term perspectives, it is so interesting to notice that this sector is far from being a motionless economic player.

CHAPTER 1

THE GLOBAL AGRIBUSINESS SYSTEM

The agro-production mentioned in the introduction strongly evolved. People gradually organized themselves another way to produce and consume their food. In classifying jobs whether they are "production" or "services," it is possible to accentuate the phenomenon of the increase of activities in the service sector that occurred in the world economic dynamics: more than half are in services.

By analyzing the accounting figures at the international level, it is easy to notice that the agricultural supply and the equipment worldwide count millions of companies generating hundreds of billion dollars of sales; the agribusiness also gathers as many companies for billions of dollars of turnover; while the processing industries add up even more businesses a gigantic turnover in billions of dollars.

Other services would consist of hundreds of thousands of companies. The final food expenditure amounts to several hundred billions on average by industrialized countries, which is sold by two to three hundred thousand companies on average per country. The three quarters of sales are the fact of distribution, and the remaining quarter comes from catering.

Some older statistics allow us to detail the nature of the companies of this group. In the agricultural supply in the strict sense, most of the microcompanies disappeared and the sector is dominated by a strong oligopoly of a handful of companies. We will come back on the difficulties of enumeration of the agricultural companies. But the majority is unipersonal, whereas a certain number of companies make the two thirds of agro-production.

There is an important artisanal sector of agribusiness, while we count some companies with more than ten employees throughout the world. Forty percent of the sales is realized by companies of more than five-hundred employees in the world, who gather 30 percent of the staff of the sector; 55 percent of the sales by small- and medium-sized enterprises (SMEs) from ten to five hundred employees, which corresponds to 50 percent of the staff of the sector; 5 percent of the sales is the fact of very small companies of less than ten employees who add up 20 percent of the staff of the sector.

The international distribution remains characterized by numerous small shops in every country and by a very strong oligopoly of a number of groups. It is the ascendancy of craftsmanship that marks the restoration, where there are, however, some big specialized groups. How are these figures going to evolve the next years?

Concerning the relative weight of products and growth observed on food markets, "where to find some growth?" is leitmotif of the professionals. Seventy-five percent of the market in the developed countries corresponds to mass-market products which growth is low: 0–1 percent a year. The "greedy" products represent 20 percent of the global market and grow between 5 and 10 percent, whereas "healthy" products, in the developed countries, progress from 15 to 20 percent a year partially for a market share of 5 percent.

Crossing these observations, it is necessary to note that "basic items" with much segmented organoleptic characteristics, come from diversified territorial origins and are the object of mass industrial processes; the social history of the product is often irrelevant except sometimes because of marketing and the price remains low. Local products worldwide are much "typified" with a clearly specified territorial origin and result from a "normalized" craft process; the social history of the product is very present and the price is high. The "innovative" products in this domain have relatively neutral tastes and the territorial origin is generally unimportant. However, they result from an advanced technology and if, by definition, their history does not exist, and their price is very high. We see indeed, the possible strategies of development appear. However, these considerations are essentially specific to each country, regional at most.

Four stages of evolution exist therein and in the domains of agriculture, handwork, agro-industry and services. By comparing different production systems all over the world (both on the historical and geographical plan) considering the repartition, in the purchase price of food products, the value resulting from producers, manufacturers and from services, we can determinate two distinct consumption modes: at home or out-of-home dining. Four stages of evolution so are to be defined: agriculture (self-subsistence, poverty); handwork: differentiation, urbanization; agribusiness (production and mass production); and agro-tertiary (service and segmentation).

To illustrate the share of operators in the final price paid by consumers and make it more accurate in the analysis, we can refer to the following examples: the least developed countries such as Tanzania and Bangladesh are at the agricultural stage, and at the artisanal level, there are low-income developing countries such as Bolivia, or with an intermediary income such as Brazil; the countries of the Organization for Economic Co-operation and Development are the agribusiness stage. In developed countries in general, added value of agribusiness and of the industry of agro-production are equal and the share of catering was then 20 percent, other countries then are still at the agro-tertiary stage.

We anticipate that the agro-tertiary stage cannot be generalized at the planetary level; however, most of the observers claim that the major part of the developed countries will follow the agro-tertiary model. In reality, nothing is less safe, because the orientation of the food request depends on a very important number of factors. Some are under the direct influence of the actors, whereas the others depend on strategies adopted by public authorities: prices, taxes, subsidies; information, training; innovation; organization; governance at the level of the company, in that of the States, and in the supranational scale.

However, it is not easy to find a way in all these groups, especially as the "distance" increases between the production of the agricultural raw materials and the consumption of the food made from them. For a long time we favored a linear representation worldwide; the origin being the farmer producer, and the consumer destroyer of the final product.

We used the concept of vertical coordination of flows, that of the sector, which connects by contract each actor. Today, the image of food chain is often adopted, in particular by the logisticians who speak of "supply chain" to call up all the connections uniting the supplies necessary for the delivered product to satisfy the demand of the final customer. This one has become the king, sometimes, it is the concentric vision that is preferred.

Therefore, the consumer would not be the terminal element of the chain anymore. From now, he would be on in the center and the "shelves" would connect him to each operator of the food set: agribusiness, agro-food supply, agribusiness, agribusiness industries, logistics, distribution channels, and professional and public institutions.

Each of these evocations provides a descriptive representation that highlights such or such actor; and it is true that, in certain countries, at least where the agribusiness was very "valued" to a certain extent, these were often considered as the "central core." It resulted in "farm-centric" designs, not very explanatory of phenomena and contemporary stakes. Doubtless, it is necessary to observe it from another angle to discover something other than an "upstream" (animal feed, chemistry, fertilizers, phytosanitary and animal health para-chemistry, oil products, machinery and agricultural equipment, building and civil engineering, and transports and supply services) and a downstream output of agribusiness (Food industries reaching the final consumer via the mass-market retailing) or nonfood (wood, furniture, paper, cardboard, textiles, clothing, biofuels, and "green chemistry"). The idea of a "system," unfortunately a little more complicated, would allow a more realistic approach to the mechanisms of functioning.

The "system" approach, widely used in the life sciences and in the social sciences, allows to understand in particular that any modification of an element modify other elements.

Thus, the agribusiness system can be considered as a finalized system (satisfaction of the function of food consumption); a biological system (due to the nature of its products); an opened system (multiple relations with basic natural resources: earth, climate, socioeconomic, and cultural environment); a complex system (several hundred thousand millions of economic agents involved, in the agribusiness world, the agro-production industry, the distribution, the peripheral services, and industries); a partially determined system (the production system is influenced by the random variations of the agro-climatic environment and the volatility of the physical and financial markets); a system with multiple centers of order (companies and governmental institutions); a mixed regulation system (the market, the public authorities, and the international agreements).

The "effective" system is the one described at the beginning of this chapter and summarized as the production of agricultural raw materials; transformation, industrial or craft, of raw materials; packaging of consumed products whether fresh or transformed; distribution of products with differentiated incorporation of services; logistics (transport and storage, transshipments); manufacturing of goods and services necessary for the network described (peripheral activities: machines and equipment, packaging, insurances and financing, research and development, training and regulations).

This first "effective" subsystem works thanks to the subsystem of "information," symbolized by bar codes, to be replaced by "intelligent" labels (radio frequency identification). These new information and communication technologies accelerate the connections between the actors, especially between the industrialists and the retailers. "Loyalty cards" complete the device. More than a way to pay, they are a tool to know the consumer behavior in detail. They authorize very fine analyses, and more than daily, of the sales of stores. So, it is possible to anticipate the programming of assembly lines, to optimize transport on purchases and on sales, to minimize stocks, to synchronize commercial transactions, to decrease the financial expenses on circulating capital, etc.

The performance of the actors of the effective system will depend more and more on their ability to enter the information system. Here, there is a very important field of exploration, in particular for the producers, who could free themselves from the distance to the final consumer. The other way around, it is all the stakes in the traceability, thus in the safety and in the responsibility, that is raised.

The subsystem of decision weaves many relations with the first effective subsystem and the subinformation system. It is extremely diverse, reacting to the market signals (mainly the prices), obeying in — or putting pressure on — professional organizations (it is lobbying: historically; agricultural professional organizations are very numerous and very multiplied, from the European level to the local level; changes along the lines of simplification are to be expected).

The subsystem of decision must respect the legal standards as well or the rules that voluntarily prevail on the professionals, in the domains of quality and sanitary safety, for example.

Institutions intervene strikingly in these relations, in particular through the competition law. Thus, we can recall that the merger acquisitions in the sector only authorized on certain conditions not to create an abuse of dominant position, or that the new groups so established were obliged to get rid of several stores in the zones where industrial networks became too dense.

And, naturally, we could evoke the recent modifications concerning the commercial practices (prohibition of resale at a loss or "false" commercial cooperation).

By successive images, a conceptualization of the agribusiness system was elaborated on one hand and, on the other hand, it is now possible to get an idea of its processes of functioning.

We "touch" its representation and we are ready to admit that it invents its own transformations to remain viable. Sensitive areas appear where unpredictable evolutions cannot be predicted but can be approached by likely scenarios.

None of them will occur exactly as imagined; however, the simple effort of mental construction required to build the scenarios prepared for action. And this one has more chances to be relevant in front of the effective modifications that will arise.

Some fields appear as criticisms. The subsystem "agro-food supply" is particularly concerned by the environmental aspects: "chemical" agribusiness, pesticides, genetically modified organism (GMO), etc.

The model of agro-production is called out: Is the productivity agribusiness sustainable and can the producers get a decent income? Naturally, these questions concern rich countries most of the time; they are more rarely at the global "systematic" level, mainly because it is not easy to design. Nevertheless, an answer is required, because partisan forces are at work.

The food safety worries transformers (craftsmen and industrialists) as well as the retailers, whatever are their formats: hypermarkets, supermarkets, minimarkets, hard discounters, independent craftsmen, and operators of the short marketing circuits for farm and food products.

The consumers, also taxpayers, worry about their health, so, consequently, as public authorities. They worry about the sustainability of their culinary heritage or are alarmed by the standardization of foodstuffs.

In brief, a real public debate takes shape, and thus a strategic and economic debate. It is established, for everyone, in the local sphere and quickly reaches "global" considerations no one gets.

Nobody can, however, extract of this problem. It is at the same time a very intimate problem (what do I risk by ingesting such food?).

And in the most desperate cases (how to get me food?), a collective problem (even the agri-food producer feeds on food from elsewhere!).

The agribusiness system of countries, the regional agribusiness system and the global agribusiness system are interconnected.

And they are all influenced by the tension of the relationships connecting the demographic pressure (generated by people themselves) with the availability and in the renewal of the resources they need to live. To live well or to survive.

Will the world adapt itself to the new stakes in the agribusiness? Can the innovative modes of consumption be generalized at the world level?

CHAPTER 2

THE DEMOGRAPHY AND RESOURCES

The agribusiness system's primary function is to feed the population from the natural resources available on the planet. In reality, population and resources belong to the same ecosystem: they interact. They are forces of nature whose functioning must be understood so that people can ensure their own sustainability by protecting the whole viability. Thus, it is necessary to look for the dynamic balance of these forces. What happens at the demographic plan, globally and locally?

Can we understand these evolutions to adopt proper behaviors for the future? We cannot constantly observe the indefinite increase of our population or not react, act, and anticipate in front of meteorological and climatic variations. Or remain anxious by observing the progressive exhaustion of the fossil fuels, the water, or the lands which we use to make our food.

Demographers understand better and better how our populations evolve. Malthus feared that the population grows much faster than the food. And the racing of figures might generate fears. Shall we soon be several billion? How are we going to survive? Will humanity be able to survive?

Today, according to demographers, the world population should stabilize around 2050. And, humanity ages, the birth rate decreases, the Earth population increases slower than planned. In

2040, 21 percent of the human beings will be more than sixty years old, and, as with relief: the planet will not witness a demographic explosion.

We will think well about our food problem if we report some of the well-known mechanisms. We are all familiar with the age pyramid, because we were able to observe our own populations at a moment when fertility and birth rate were simultaneously brought up.

In reality, fertility and mortality evolve and fall with the "progresses." Thus, "transition" takes place from a population with a high fertility and mortality to a population with a low fertility and mortality. As the demographic transition becomes true, the pyramid deforms, takes the shape of a cylinder, then that of an inverted cone. Naturally, all the populations do not evolve similarly and, according to their degree of evolution, they do not face the same problems.

As in many phenomena of the "living," the world population follows a curve "S": at first there is a progressive increase, then a progressive braking, reach of a peak, then a decrease. The maximum of the demographic growth of the world population was reached during the decade 1960s. There was progressive adjustment of the fertility over the mortality: This one decreased at first by entailing an important natural increase; now, the birth rate decreases, so that the world population will reach a maximum toward 2050, then will decrease. It is also very important to note that some countries have already begun this decrease: In five years, seventeen developed countries became depopulated!

The map of the world populations changes: the industrialized world ages, the "differential demographic pressures" cause migrations, so many characteristics, which are going to press on the quantity of food to be supplied according to the geographical zones. So, we obviously see the very slow acceleration of the origin taking shape; then are needed less and less years so that the world population increases by a billion. From this century, the progress decreases: we are around the inflection point of the "S" curve; we began the slowing down phase to reach the summit of the curve in approximately fifty years. Then, the population should stabilize and probably decrease.

It is necessary to understand that it is the economic and social development that conditioned the reduction in the mortality at first, then that of the fertility after. The "development" appears as the key in the limitation of populations. Let us insist: to limit populations, they should reach development. But it emerges that a modification between the age groups, does not miss to influence the specific nutritional needs of given population, and thus, on the production of the necessary food, and consequently on the agro-production.

We shall also understand that there is a brief period for every population during which the proportion of adults from fifteen to sixty-five years increases significantly with regard to that of the young people and elderly: it is a "window" during which "more" people can get involved in directly productive tasks. From it will result specific qualitative nutritional needs, just as much as particular modes of food consumption. Naturally, the consequences are immediate on the requests of the food, system, especially on distribution, on the agricultural and food industries and on agribusiness.

The transitions cover specific mechanisms which apply to demography, to health, to food, and to economy. We have just understood that the "demographic transition," now well known by demographers, governs the quantitative and qualitative modifications of the population's needs, thus the geographical zones of the world. Other phenomena also bear the name of "transition." We talk about "sanitary transition" when the infectious and acute diseases are replaced by the chronic and degenerative diseases, and we know that cancers, cardiovascular diseases, diabetes, and obesity — which are a part of the second — are completely related to food. Moreover, we name food "transition" the phenomenon that sees, in diets, animal-derived calories substituted by an increasing proportion of vegetable calories. Finally, we are familiar with the processes of "transition of economies toward capitalism."

All these "transitions," which characterize demography, health, food, and economy, will help us understand better the connections with agribusiness, at the time of the globalization. But let us stay in the demography. Doubtless, for a long time, the specialists of the agribusiness will be recruited rather within the families of the developers now in place. But, eventually in the long term, this traditional model of recruitment risks itself, otherwise to disappear, at least to lose its exclusivity. So will be born — in the middle of the difficulties that have to be planned to warn them — a world without peasant particularism, that is, an agribusiness system without farmers.

Where is the world today? The disappearance of producers would take place in the next years, if the demographic forecasts were based on a linear logic. This logic is the one that everyone uses spontaneously when wondering about the future of the agricultural population; it feeds the concerns of producers and, among them, young people. The reference population consists of the "professional listed exploitations": they represent 95 percent of the agricultural added value, the 92 percent of the land tax, and 59 percent of exploitations (which means that there are several microexploitations and that the use of figures must be careful).

In reality, demography is not linear: it follows an "S" curve having exceeded its summit and "energy toward the descent." After the summit, the descent accelerates (rural–urban migration), then slowed down to be almost stopped now. It is the end of a phenomenon of "demographic transition." Supposing that there are no more installations during several years, it is an important flow of exiting professionals that should be necessary to notice, bringing the number of farms to an optimum in the coming years. But there will be installations on farms which size and definition will have varied.

To understand what may happen in the future, some elements seem essential. First of all, the fixed asset in agribusiness is constant for some time, which means that the "agricultural farm" is stabilized. On the other hand, age groups contain approximately the same number of producers, from thirty-five to fifty-five years old. If the "global agricultural farm" was distributed between the producers from thirty-five to fifty-five years, and if there were every year so many incomers as of outgoing, the situation would have actually been stabilized. But the reality is obviously a bit different: we settle down on average from twenty-two to thirty-five years old and we leave the agribusiness from fifty to sixty-five years old.

Besides, two phenomena had a disturbing effect: the offer of farms was scarce a few years ago because of, on one hand, the "hollow" in the generations of the World War II and, on the other hand, the early retirements which took place these last years. These early retirements freed lands, which were especially used for enlargements, to return the "viable" exploitations. Thus, the possibilities of installations were reduced.

The land offer should go back up very quickly. But the not agricultural pressure on the land tax increases besides... Every buyer has his logic: community, farmer, urban... But it is clear that it is the urban that eventually prevail, and their logic of all residential is not very compatible with the maintenance of a dynamic agribusiness able to ensure tomorrow's world, food, and energy independence. Thus, it deeply changes the territorial and landscape balances.

Would there be enough candidates to enter agribusiness? One can think, since the farms have become globally viable and have been modernized, that there will be a transmission rate from fathers to the most important sons — during the successions. But it is not counting on the fact that other children may be interested in a family capital, become important, and complicate the case; neither, on the fact that the job of farmers is not only a technical act, easy to learn "on the job," like many nonproducers — that is to say, the vast majority of the world's population — imagine it.... This profession is, moreover, becoming very sophisticated in terms of technology and management. So much so that many young producers' sons may not "feel capable" (note that about a quarter are now "senior technicians").

Thus, at least two points must be solved simultaneously: how to facilitate the assignment? And how to resume a real business? A real company with characteristics however original: the revenues are partly rents. Single payment entitlements, paid annually, are largely independent of the quantities produced.

These points, already difficult to understand, will have to be explained to citizens who are far from imagining what has become of the business of agribusiness, while there is an unprecedented movement of city dwellers who are rediscovering the "green" (biological). Things are going pretty well because there has been some balance between the extraordinary productivity efforts in agribusiness and the labor needs of reconstruction and industrialization. Despite a widening gap between rural and urban incomes, it seems that the situation of rural people is improving in absolute value. The real danger for the world is not the increase of the disparities; it would be that a drop in growth dismisses the unemployment of migrant workers. It is necessary to remember that the internal movements of population were channeled by the "sectorial" strategies and by the concerns of the distribution of growth. Today, the population increases three times as fast in the small municipalities than in the biggest.

This return in the countryside is obviously not a return of the producers and it raises specific problems: Is the world going to generate a kind of continuum of suburbs? Do we want these standardized village dormitories? Do we really want of these traffic circles and these shopping districts? Do we accept that one municipality out of two no longer have a convenience store? And, to shop which one — of the city dweller or the countryman makes most kilometers by car? Who generates most greenhouse gases? In brief, does not the individual desire to return to the countryside generate collective behavior responsible for climatic modifications and for the degradation of natural resources? And what is the part of agribusiness in these modifications?

Times change: our planet is dedicated, before fifty years, to the same fate as the Easter Island, which its inhabitants destroyed, despite their high degree of civilization. Are not we destroying the planet? In any case, the humanity modifies the climate by its greenhouse gas emissions. Over a century, the global warming is manifested by a "gap" to the north of approximately 500 km. In any case, the droughts and the summer heat waves accentuate water restrictions and the competition for this scarce resource, at least temporarily and in certain zones. The debate is easy to instigate, and the agribusiness is quickly pointed, in particular about the irrigated corn.

At the global level, the growth of population and the evolution of climate modify the risks of water shortage. And as the agribusiness uses 73 percent of the fresh water (against 21 percent for the industry and 6 percent for the domestic users), the latter is particularly concerned. So, certain countries, like China, rather than to irrigate their own productions, prefer to stock up on the market of cereals: it is easier to transport the wheat than the water necessary for its culture (4500 L of water, that is, 4.5 tons, are needed to produce 1 kg of rice, against 1500 L of water, that is, 1.5 tons, to produce 1 kg of wheat), whereas water is more profitable somewhere else in the industry.

What leads to conclude that the lack of water is going to boost agricultural exchanges? Here is a way of considering the problem of the water as a subject of conflict, but maybe not completely as an opportunity of cooperation. Let us not forget what became of the Aral Sea, which served to irrigate cotton plantations: Uzbekistan and Turkmenistan were militarily in confrontation on this matter; Turkey and Syria oppose about the Euphrates; Jordan and Israel quarrel regularly for the water of the Jordan. And what to say about the Nile, on which life depends in Egypt and in Ethiopia; as well as of South America, which holds a quarter of the world reserves of water and gathers only a little more than 5 percent of the population. We can also be taken aback by the fact that 5 percent of the development aid is dedicated to the water, against 25 percent in telecommunications. What means that the drinking water is well worth the mobile phone? As we see it, everything is not possible at the same time.

Is the public really conscious that water is "the" the most critical problem, before energy and oil? Water and oil which the agribusiness consumes. The agribusiness consumes some oil. Yet, the agro-production must follow the food demand, which has to follow the demographic progress. It ensues from it that the consumption of oil has to increase to solve the problem of the food, generating pollution and global warming, whereas we approach the exhaustion of the known reserves.

We see that it is necessary "to change the game," if we want to find a solution. For that purpose, it is necessary to understand at least how the agribusiness consumes some oil on one hand and, on the other hand, to examine if it is possible to substitute another energy source to oil, in agribusiness as in the other sectors.

In industrialized countries, the agricultural revolution was based on the tractor (and therefore, fuel), on phytosanitary chemistry from oil and from fertilizers stemming from some gas (as nitrogen), and on deposits of phosphate or potassium hydroxide. In developing countries, the "green revolution" led to the increase of the agro-production. On the technical plan, it defines itself as an agribusiness irrigated by floods, using varieties of rice and wheat in short straw, in high yields, consuming fertilizers and phytosanitary chemical ones, and often using — but not always tillers. The results were remarkable as for the production, but the effects were also very serious pollutions, grounds.

In both cases, it is a question of reducing the wastes and the level of intensity of inputs: the reasoned agribusiness. Besides, agronomists progressed in the understanding of biological mechanisms: it is not only a question of bringing artificial fertilizers to the "climate-ground-plant" system anymore. By understanding the biological mechanisms which follow one another during the operations of production, they finalized the concept "of technical route" that ends in increases of yield using practices inspired by the biological agribusiness (whose internal processes were not well known).

To simplify, we can admit that the reasoned agribusiness limit pollutions and economic charges, while protecting the yields, which is particularly interesting in the countries where high levels are already reached. We can also admit that countries that used the green revolution can reason at the same time with their agribusiness and make the yields progress by using techniques considering the whole ecosystem: it is a double green revolution.

Yet, it is globally necessary to increase the yields, as the available cultivable areas are not sufficient. Some claim that, just because the agro-production increased slightly faster than the population in the last observations made that there is enough to feed the population in the future. It is besides without considering the fact that cultivating on new areas has an ecological cost (the destruction of the primary forest, for example).

It is finally without considering the fact that the current practices can deteriorate the soil and make them lose their fertility. It is over and above the fact that numerous surfaces are removed from culture or from nature. The urbanization, the construction of roads, and destruction of the forest ... decrease the total ability of plants in the photosynthesis, that is, the capacity of the planet to use sunlight to produce energy falls! These phenomena are global. But the demographic pressure, the tensions on water, and the availability of lands are very variable from a point to another one of the globes. It results from it that we cannot talk about "the agribusiness"; on the contrary, we must consider the "agribusiness" of the world and admit, however, that they are not completely independent of each other, the movements of balancing being made by the transport of food or the migrations of populations.

Moreover, the expensive oil made coal more competitive, the development of solar and wind energy is in progress, the future of the gas seems assured and we reconsider with more interest nuclear power. And to mention that tankers do everything to value their productions in the face of the rise of biofuels.

Is it really the end of black gold? Do we attend a new episode of green oil? Knowing that agribusiness can produce some energy in the form of biofuels relieves the spirit, at least in first analysis. The solution of biofuels seems twice positive: on one hand, it brings a substitute to oil and, on the other hand, it is an immediately available solution to reduce CO_2 emissions. Indeed, the consumption of biofuels is only releasing in the atmosphere the same CO_2 the biomass took from the growth of plants.

But it is necessary to look at it closer. At the global level and at the horizon two miles fifty, he (it) is not obvious of the whole that the agribusiness can supply biofuels besides the food (supply). As some people say it, "you must choose: drive or eat!"

Attempts of budgeted balance sheets exist. Bases and reasoning must be discussed and deepened. However, before 2050, agribusiness will have massively produced biofuels: in Brazil, in the United States, in France, in Canada; but also in India, in China, and in Russia. For the gasoline sector, the sources are beets, cereal, or sugar cane. For the diesel sector, it is at first about colza and sunflower. Then the lignocellulosic cultures (the wood giving the BTL, "biomass to liquid"). The gas and the coal will also have given their contribution with "clean" ("appropriate") technologies: GTL, "gas to liquids," and CTL, "coal to liquids."

Gradually, a regular review of technologies and the knowledge in all the fields will lead to reconsider the global and local assessments' "food and energy" and, consequently, the request of agribusiness. Subbalances are going to change: on one side, the sector of gasoline/ethanol and, on the other one, the diesel/diester sector. The evolution of car manufacturers is so much to consider than that of the refining capacities of tankers.

Besides, industrialists will request agribusiness for biomaterials: industrial objects — partially intended for automobiles, but not only — will be more and more developed from linen, from hemp, or from the starch of cereal or potato — whereas the use of the oil and its by-products will modify and "green chemistry" will progress.

We think first of the vegetable productions, as shown almost everywhere in the world by the "agricultural resources" pole of competitiveness, aimed at being global. However, the animal productions can contribute too: it is about using some parts of oil and animal fats of cattle-rearing areas to produce biodiesel.

Besides, next to the big projects, more reduced initiatives — but led with passion — were established to transform directly on the farm, oleaginous plants in agricultural fuel. No doubt that we will learn from the experiences: evolution of the motorizations, but also use of oil cakes, extraction residues... On this matter, it is interesting to note that some of the oil presses manufacturers are small and medium-sized companies — in the orbit of groups, essentially working in Africa — formerly press specialist to extract the oil of cotton seeds... We also find with amusement these purely individual initiatives, which consist in stocking up with salad oil to hard discounters for the needs of personal vehicles.

As it is still seen here, it is absolutely necessary to have a global view to appreciate the role of agribusiness: world subbalances of the oil and energy capacities; world subbalances of the agricultural capacities supply food, biofuels, and biomaterials; world subbalances that opened the industrial fallow and thus, allowed the first experiments of biodiesel...

These progressive modifications of balances will lead to adjust — all over the world and regionally — the necessary areas for the energy production of agribusiness. Maybe, as it will be meant to dedicate surfaces equivalent to those, essential to the animal driving force, before the agricultural revolution!

We are not there still for the limits which we perceive. In the upcoming years, some of these limits will be pushed away, whereas others will doubtless appear. Also, is it a pragmatic and realistic behavior that we must adopt? We must deal with the world as it goes; consider the reflections of the most serious "birds of woes" to act with caution; encourage the most creative to innovate, to fall in an optimism that will release the scientific effort; and continuously update our technical knowledge.

In fact, next to several well-established mechanisms, we discover that some are hardly predictable, like the evolution of the climate. But especially, we become aware that our world is "finite" and that it is a gigantic system, on which human actions are very significant. If it calls for precaution, it is especially about being responsible and take part in the regulation of the system. This awareness is vital: our system must be renewed. We must get to know it not to cause irreversible consequences; we certainly need to have repaired actions and, when we almost lose viability, select actions whose consequences are reversible. We become completely responsible for our global ecosystem.

Agribusiness is in the center of our system of the "living"; there is no "primitive nature" anymore today. Agribusiness thus appears as determining in the reception of the solar energy essential to the biosphere human beings influence very significantly. Producers or not, we must all, for the general interest, take part in the decisions of orientation influencing agribusiness. We know that we participate all in a unique global system of interconnected elements, what does not exclude the diversity of local situations. So, by symmetry, every local decision must be taken at a global point of view.

The densities of population are very variable. Their map, however, is not confounded with that of the zones favorable to the agribusiness, neither with that of the water resources or energy. It means that economies, differentiated according to geography, will keep their originality, in spite of the homogenizing tendencies of globalization. It also implies that the social organizations will maintain their proper marks. Here, the fight against poverty will be a priority. There, we shall modify the use of the water by improving the techniques of irrigation or by modifying the agronomic practices in pluvial zone of agribusiness.

Here, the scientific programs will favor researches on the fixation of the atmospheric nitrogen by plants. Somewhere else, the progress on paedogenesis will be favored, to clean up, to repair grounds, or even to generate it from the source rock.

Under other latitudes, the investments in desalination of the seawater that will come in first. But over there, the wastewater treatment or the use of the organic waste (animal and human) will have the priority. In this zone, the forest should be favored, instead of installing a corn–soya system. And, in this zone, we focus on the feeding mode: eating vegetables consumes less agricultural surface than eating products of animal origin.

So, while taking refuge with magic behavior, we shall find the solutions: “let’s hope that it lasts!”

Also, only criticism is not sufficient: proved proposals must be discussed. And surrounding walls must be arranged for the confrontation and the implementation of solutions. So, the shortages will be ruled out, the innovation favored, and the growth directed. We are not anymore in a bipolar, vast world where the stake in the agricultural and food development was to avoid revolts, even revolutions, risking to make peoples fall over to one or the other camp. In our unique and finite biosphere, the regulations should be discussed. And it is up to each of the actors to take part in meeting the challenge of sustainable agribusinesses.

CHAPTER 3

BEING LIBERAL AND RULE?

The tensions of "forces of nature" are not the only ones to happen. And the pressure on agribusiness doubles, when the institutional discussions are sine die put back: the agricultural aids cause the failure of the liberalization of trade. Never commercial cycles had gone so far in agriculture, before ending suddenly. So, by the cycles intended to favor the activity of the poor countries are suspended, quite logically with millennium development goals. In first position, the United Nations put the "fight against poverty": Halve the proportion of the population whose income is lower than a dollar a day and half malnutrition.

So, to the question of whether to stick liberalization? It is important to emphasize that the agricultural productivity of the "already rich" cannot lead to the food sovereignty of the "still poor." We saw that the agro-production and the world food evolved slightly faster than the population during the last fifty years. But we count two billion people who suffer from hunger and 850 million being hungry, mainly in developing countries. Yet, most of these are food producers, poor farmers.

How to explain that producing farmers cannot afford food? To understand that, it is necessary to note that the gap in productivity is around one to one thousand between the "manual" culture the least successful, practiced in the developing world, for example, and the most successful motorized culture, practiced in the rich countries, for example (to fix the ideas, it is admitted that the gap in productivity between "manual" culture and the culture with animal drive was from one to ten).

Ten quintals of cereal produced in one year by a man in Africa: a man working on one hectare and obtaining a ten-quintal yield. Ten thousand quintals a year for a man in Quebec: a worker out of a hundred hectares producing hundred quintals a hectare. The gap is the same for animal productions: an African farmer with a milking cow gets 1000 L a year, when a New Zealand breeder milks more than one hundred cows and gets 10,000 mL a year. On one side, the majority of farmers work manually only with tools, without fertilizer or phytosanitary; on the other side, a minority benefited from the agricultural revolution and use tractors, selected seeds, fertilizer, and phytosanitary.

Productivity gains obtained by the agricultural revolution and by the green revolution were enormous during the last fifty years, so that the prices of farm products were divided by four or five depending on products and countries. The operating revenues dropped, and we saw that there is a smaller part of professional operations in industrialized countries. Besides, further to the liberalization of the capital movements, massive investments were realized, in particular in the big exploitations of Latin America or the Eastern countries. The productivity so obtained has its compensation: reduction of employment, the low incomes, the malnutrition that is the contraction of the internal market of farm products, and the increase of the available quantities on the export at a low price.

These sale prices are much lower than cost prices obtained by the majority of the producers of the world producers. And these prices, through the international markets, compete with the local productions, which sale prices must follow up, thus, becoming lower than the production costs. We understand that the incomes from the local agribusiness do not contribute to development. Among the poorest, these incomes do not even allow them to feed themselves properly. In the rich countries, where there are no regulating mechanisms, the producers would have no income or a negative income. What the rich countries cannot accept, because of their sovereignty; they want their agricultural independence to ensure a safe and regular supply for their processing companies and food retailing.

However, the agricultural markets are volatile: the law of supply and demand does not apply in a classic way. The agricultural productions are fluctuating in quantity and quality (climate, diseases), whereas the capacities of food consumption are relatively stiff in volume, related to disposable income. Price changes are amplified: they collapse as soon as the quantities exceed those necessary for consumption, whereas they increase, making food very expensive, if quantities are lacking. For the poorest of the producer's consumer, it goes off their survival there. Agricultural prices cannot be the basis of their food safety or their development. And the reduction of price instability is the focus of agricultural strategies aimed at satisfying both consumers and producers.

The low purchasing power of half of humanity limits global food consumption in this regard. Today, half of the world's population is made up of producers' consumers: three billion have less than two dollars a day and more than a billion have less than a dollar a day. This weakness of the purchasing power of half of humanity limits the world food consumption, far below its needs and far below the possibilities of development of production, which is literally restrained by the drop of agricultural prices and their instability. Thus, fostering the development of the poorest would contribute to control the evolution of the population; to produce with much improved agricultural productivity, using better production factor for sustainable development; but also, to increase the world food consumption and, consequently, the overall growth.

However, the observation of productivity differences as important as those highlighted, require to reason by subsets in the neighboring productivities and to connect these subsets between them. Real regional strategies of development should be developed. Moreover, regionalization around the world should be based on a community preference, a prerequisite for expansion, employment, and prosperity.

This principle has a universal validity for all the countries. For any regional economy, a reasonable objective would be that, by appropriate policies and for every product or group of products, a minimal percentage of the community consumption is assured by the community production, excluding any relocation.

The average value of this percentage could be 80 percent. With regard to the current situation, a fundamentally liberal arrangement would allow an effective functioning of any economy removed from all the external disorders while assuring extensive and advantageous links with all third countries. It is a major condition for the growth of developed countries, but it is especially a major condition for the development of underdeveloped countries.

It would be preferable to establish, for a rather long period, large regional agricultural common markets around the world gathering countries with relatively close agricultural productivities, and to protect them against quite import of low-priced agricultural surpluses, in order to raise agricultural price and stabilize them at a level allowing the farmers of disadvantaged areas to live off their work, to invest, and to grow. And it would be necessary to establish, if need be, food strategies not based on the sale of farm products with reduced price, but on the increase of the purchasing power of the disadvantaged buyers, by the distribution of purchase vouchers, as ... in the United States.

The developed countries have a broad experience. They know that in reality, the real choice is not between the absence of any protection and a protectionism completely isolating every national economy from the outside. It is looking for a system allowing every economy to benefit from an effective competition and from the advantages of many exchanges with the outside, but which can also protect it against all the disorders and the dysfunctions that characterize every day the global economy. Concerning the place of agribusiness in front of international institutions, it is necessary before any analysis to specify that there are at least two schools of thought. On one hand, some consider that the opening of trade is as beneficial to agribusiness as it is to other products. On the other hand, others think that agribusiness is very specific, and that the principle of the food sovereignty is essential.

This distance between both positions placed the agribusiness at the center of the discussions, which did not progress on the other points. And countries, at the end of several years, were not able to find an agreement. While for some, liberalizing trade is the key of everything, for the others, the opening of trade must be followed by conditions of all kinds.

Let us add that the developed countries are rather democracies which have budgets allowing them to lead public strategies while, at the level of developing or changing countries, the means are sorely lacking, many imbalances remaining to be corrected. In this context, the role of the international institutions in the area is limited to facilitating the trade: organization's work on lowering tariff barriers and facilitating foreign investments. They are not development organization or funding agencies. And, given the complexity of agricultural problems that must consider simultaneously all the dimensions, the limits of competence are easily affected: the World Trade Organization (WTO) for example is not the organization of the United Nations for the food and production, nor World Bank.

That is why, thanks to the suspension of the negotiations, it might be wholesome to hear the new proposals that are being elaborated. The trade liberalization of farm products involves more than agricultural trade: it risks to decrease the food sovereignty that certain countries have been able to build, whereas it prevents other from building their own food sovereignty.

Should not these organizations content to support the commercial implementation of real agricultural strategies? They would obviously be different depending on regions: responding to local specificities, they would aim at autonomy and food safety, in quantity and quality. The movement for a world organization of production has taken a step in this way. Agribusiness appeared as the "Achilles heel" of the globalization, at the same time, as it could be the key to global growth.

Why are we stuck? Why is the United States resisting any cuts in their internal production subsidies? Were the Europeans ready to lower tariffs on agricultural imports? Would emerging countries, in particular Brazil, India, and China, have agreed to lower their tariffs on industrial products? And would the poor countries have found the conditions of their economic and social takeoff?

As we know, the programs in certain regions quickly generated surpluses, what brought in direct competition with the major producing countries, to which it nibbles at market shares. And the United States chose the General Agreement on Tariffs and Trade (GATT) to summon certain producers to dismantle their refund system. The leaders of these countries will eventually accept to reopen a cycle of negotiations and to talk about agribusiness there. The principle of a global negotiation was accepted, concerning in particular services, intellectual property, investments, and production. It will further liberalize the trade of farm products. Negotiators of certain countries succeeded in ensuring that it covers all the direct and indirect measures, which refers to the American system of deficiency payments, the effect of which is to favor the agricultural exports of the United States while lowering the global costs.

The cycle will end with a very important decision: the dismantling of the variable levies. This system removed certain countries from a threshold. To override, products had to acquit an amount corresponding to the difference, variable, between the global price, also variable, and the minimum fixed. This mechanism financed areas, thus constituting reserves to support symmetrically export products through subsidies. In this "oasis," some countries developed other agricultural strategies, including guaranteed price systems. These variable levies will be converted into fixed customs duties, whose decrease was programmed. That is the way one of the main engines that led certain countries to be exporters of their surpluses is meant to stop.

Another result was to classify the supports to agribusiness according to the importance of competition distortions they produce. The production direct aids (support prices) were put in the orange box: these aids are subject to reduction. In the blue box were placed the aids allowing a control of the offer. Based on the surface, the yield, or the number of animals, these aids will decrease in time. Finally, the supports of the green box are the aids which have no effect on production or exchanges, that is which do not cause distortion of competition (agricultural and environmental measures, research aid). These aids are not subjected to an obligation of reduction.

The global domination of certain countries in agriculture was challenged by the success of a minority. It is during the Uruguay round that the Americans and their allies of the Cairns group tried to dismantle the levy system. An institution will be created at the world level to liberalize trade in general. The GATT was a kind of forum frequented by a "club of rich countries"; the organization of trade is an institution created in 1995: two thirds of the members are developing countries, who wish to use this forum to take part in balancing the world trade, in an organization where the decisions must be adopted unanimously. Next to the developed countries, emerging countries will be very offensive and the least developed countries will not bear to be "outcasts." The operation is obviously going to be laborious and to remain focused on agricultural questions. Nevertheless, certain cycle had to be that of development generally...

First, there was an opening of this cycle, then a failure of certain meetings. Then, the South came forward. Then, the main issues remained unresolved, the agricultural question slowly progressing: the conference approved the removal of all the subsidies of agricultural exports. But, the lack of agreement was preferred, the dispute on the aids to the agribusiness not being still solved.

Development will wait. At least, the development regulated by multilateral agreements, while a more uneven development could appear within the framework of bilateral agreements: What to think of multilateral agreements by big regions and between big regions? Unless the dismantling of the distortions of competition on markets starts again. Or rather, would it not be a question of decreasing the distortions of competition between the areas whose agribusinesses became "sufficient" on one hand, and to build, on the other hand, the temporary protections (necessarily on long term) necessary for the agricultural development of the least developed economic areas?

Let us take the point of view of developed countries on the distortions of competition. They are, after reforms, limited today. For example, the productions are "contained": the dairy quotas put an upper limit on the dairy production (the stocks of butter and milk powder are very low) and the fallow, by freezing part of the surface, led to reduce the stocks of cereal and to better respect the environment, as well as to experiment on the crops intended for biofuels.

The decoupling of the aids decreases the link between the production and the aids, while it strengthens the link of production with the market; the decoupling moves from aid for products to aid for farmers. Knowing that this one perceives it only if he respects the fixed standards: the ecoconditionality thus tends toward an agribusiness which considers the environment. Inside these countries, although the rate of global decoupling is now 92 percent, countries had the choice in the decoupling intensity. Some, for example, chose on the contrary, a total coupling for the herd of suckler cows, to protect the activity and the spatial planning in areas such as the Massif Central.

Concerning the exports, the refunds were considerably reduced: certain countries even went beyond the commitments made. Globally, all types of support were notified to whom it may concern, and subsidies are a public information. It is not as clear in the other industrialized countries: certain instruments used are complex or are not subject to discipline, even if they have powerful distorting effects on competition.

Since these are important points of the "agricultural dispute," it is useful to explain them briefly. Certain countries have organized boards. They are public or parapublic companies that have the monopoly of the export. Considering this characteristic, they weigh on the export prices in world markets they influence. This includes the New Zealand dairy board, the Canadian wheat board, the Australian wheat board, or the Queensland Corporation, in Australia as well.

Either export credits are made available to exporters at extremely advantageous rates and with deferred refunds: 15 percent of the Australian agricultural exports and 5 percent of the Canadian agricultural exports benefited from these export credits, supported by the public. Figures show only 2 percent for Europe and 6 percent for the United States, which by playing on the "mix product," focused their operations on wheat, which was supported by 17 percent. We can add that 19 percent of guarantees in certain countries is granted for less than a month, whereas 94 percent of guarantees granted by the others are longer than one year and sometimes can go up to ten years.

Marketing loans are a classic form of the American agricultural strategy. These aids are notified as internal support instrument, but not as an export subsidy. However, it has been demonstrated that they have a destabilizing effect on world prices, because they tend to increase the production when prices fall. Food aid is a key instrument of the American foreign strategy. As an aid, it aims at increasing export markets for the American farm products.

The emergency and development operations of the American Agency for International Development and the food for education programs are certainly very helpful. But three programs, accounting for 63 percent of the aid, are used for commercial purposes: "confessional" loans (sales on preferential conditions, very low rate, very long repayment periods); the donations from the American department of agribusiness; and the food for progress programs (other credit sale program and gifts).

Moreover, nontariff barriers are used. Emphasizing environmental policies, they are mainly used in Brazil, Argentina, New Zealand, and Australia, which stand out with three quarters of their imports covered by environmental protectionist barriers. In other developed countries, this kind of practice concerns three times fewer products than in Canada or in the United States. Finally, there is a specific practice in Argentina, which applies a 23.5 percent export tax on soya beans and oilseeds, but of only 20 percent on oil cakes and oil. It hampers the other countries crushers, for which the purchase of the raw material is made more expensive than for their Argentine competitors. But we are not going to resume all the current or suspended discussions...

It would be better to focus on developing agribusinesses in the developing world without sacrificing those in developed countries.

By remaining liberal — which is more of a humanism and a strategic position than a strict economic reasoning — and by seeking the most adapted modes of regulation, drawn from the examples of successful economic strategies.

In the recent discussions, everyone tried to calculate the order of magnitude of benefits that can be derived from the liberalization of the trade of farm products. For that purpose, economists use the data of the Global trade analysis project. It is an extremely difficult task, even if the data are simplified. In their ID3 model, the researchers of the Centre of International Co-operation in Agronomic Research for development cut the world in thirteen regions including Europe, the United States, the Mercosur ... and, finally, the "rest of the world."

They distinguished seventeen sectors: wheat, milk, oleaginous plants, forestry, the industries of agricultural production grouped into subsectors, etc. They limited the production factors to five: qualified work, unqualified work, land, natural resources and capital. If it seems extremely simplified, it is already complicated enough considering the thousands of equations to solve simultaneously. It is, however, this kind of models that are used to measure the advantages of liberalizing the markets of farm products. Furthermore, economists introduced mechanisms to consider uncertainties. The results obtained lead to the conclusion that the liberalization is much less advantageous than previously thought.

This opinion was increasingly shared by the economists of all the schools, as the global negotiations evolve. So, we can assert that the agricultural liberalization will not necessarily produce an important increase of the production, will not lead the development in the poor countries, will not significantly improve the distribution of income in the world, and will not lead to a lower food price for the benefit of consumers.

Besides the fact that these general reasonings do not consider the existence of the particular agents that companies are — which have their own behavior, experts add that it is the specific character of farm products (hazards, laws of the yields, the inelasticity of demand over prices...) which make that the "comparative advantages" — highlighted in theory to explain the benefits of the liberalization — do not really find the conditions they need to work effectively. The pure and perfect theoretical market is far too distant from the real conditions specific to the trade of farm products: this is the reason why all the countries, and especially those that have the means, namely the developed countries, set up market substitutes so that prices are the signals that guide the microeconomic behavior of producers, transformers and consumers. In this regard, people's experiences are extremely valuable: the study of agricultural strategies, and especially the conditions in which they were implemented, as well as that of the results obtained, are at least as important as the study of the laws of markets and that of the limits of the ranges of validity in which these laws get closer enough to the conditions of the reality.

The role of everyone is indisputable, globally: the international institutions have to play a role, even if they deserve to be criticized, heavily sometimes. The benefits of the WTO are recognized and each and every one will measure its utility of frame in front of the disputes, which will not miss to explode if bilateralism gets over multilateralism. That is why it is very important to relieve the WTO of problems it is not used to and which have nevertheless taken the first place within it, until it leads to inefficiency. It is necessary to save the "soldier" or the "WTO arbitrator," to optimize exchanges globally, by allowing to propose the modalities respecting the specific characters of farm products.

The MOMA (Mouvement pour une Organisation Mondiale de I' Agriculture) could help. It was created to promote a system of regulation of agricultural markets in the respect for the economic, social, and environmental balances. It produced studies showing that the current decision-making systems and decision tools (economic models, methods and basis of negotiations) no longer respond to the challenges of agribusiness for the future of humanity in terms of meeting the increasing food and nonfood needs; of the fight against poverty; of economic growth and development of countries. Thus, and contrary to the assumptions of the international institutions, a liberalization of the exchanges without the safeguard of agribusiness does not improve the economic situation of the poorest countries at all. On the contrary, it weakens them and favors countries having sometimes inconvenient, guaranteed incomes (immense territories, nonexistent social welfare, embrittlement of the environment) which, alone, can never meet an increasing demand for food and nonfood.

The main reason why liberalization does not produce the expected effects in the farming sector is because agribusiness is a strategic and specific branch of the economic sector. The strategic character of agribusiness is widely admitted by the vast majority of countries: can we imagine a country which is not able to produce enough food to feed its population? This country would be subjected to an international pressure. So, when we talk about agribusiness, we really talk about the safety of countries. The specific character is mainly due to the very strong volatility of the prices (prices), which cannot be found in any other economic sector. This characteristic is the "grain of sand" that stops the mechanics of liberalization and calls for regulation.

In response to these deficiencies and threats, several personalities from the agricultural and not agricultural industry joined the MOMA. Because its principles and the missions assigned to it correspond to universal values: promote a system of regulation of the agricultural markets on a global scale, in the respect of the economic, social and environmental equilibrium; favor the development of the exchanges as far as they contribute to improve the condition of all the producers, in particular the developing countries, and to optimize the supply security for all the countries; strengthen the research potential, the capacities of investment, productivity, employment of agricultural activities and the agro-production, in order to constantly improve the satisfaction and the safety of consumers; to fight against speculative drifts and the excessive supports distorting the functioning of markets at the expense of a sustainable development by creating a model of alert and risk assessment, develop any action of information and raising awareness allowing the international institutions and the national public authorities to take the adequate measures to regulate the world markets of farm products.

This structure is not opposed to any existing international organization, but aims at being the essential complement that is missing today. It is indeed in the perspective of harmonizing hardly compatible objectives: the fight against poverty, whose terms are described by the Millennium round; the liberalization of trade covered by international agreements; sustainable development and the environmental protection. For that purpose, it is necessary to build a global governance of agribusiness, and defined three pillars that will enable it to reach this goal while respecting the constraints of transparency, credibility, and responsibility that such a mission implies.

The model of the new agricultural regulations, the first pillar of the future global agricultural governance, will supply a decision-making tool, adapted to agribusiness, for all the negotiators and the international decision makers. It is indeed considered that it is urgent to build a new international agricultural economic model, more realistic and more credible than the conventional models, in particular that of the World Bank, the Research Institute for Food and Agricultural Strategies.

It should be noted, in particular, that these models: consider that the supply perfectly matches the demand, and therefore totally neglect the impact of the climatic factors, the phenomena of speculation and storage; suppose that the demand is totally elastic with regard to prices (will you eat twice as much if prices are halved?); do not include preferential agreements, yet essential for developing countries. And, of the member countries of the organization of trade, only nine, trade without preferential agreements; do not consider other variables interacting with the farming sector: energy, transport, sanitary regulations, environmental requirements, exchange rates...

The model which rests on a "systemic" approach and a modular architecture, consists of a central economic module of general balance, around which revolve seven satellite modules corresponding to seven criteria that any fair international agricultural model must respect, but which none respects at the moment.

So, model: estimate the level of dependence on the outside; takes into account the climatic risks and market risks; measure the effects on the poverty of the liberalization of the international agricultural exchanges; takes into account underdevelopment trapdoors led by the poverty on the future generations in developing countries; estimate the impact of the liberalization of international agricultural exchanges on the capacity of agricultural innovation and agro-production, and of its equitable sharing; join environment into the modeling of international exchanges; Takes into account sustainable development and the future of the planet, linking agricultural exchanges with global changes, that is with the climate change, biodiversity and desertification issues.

The international evaluation and rating agency, the second pillar of the global agricultural governance, along with social, environmental, or ethical rating agencies, provides key indicators of the various agricultural markets that will serve as a basis for all three of its assigned missions: simulate, estimate and note, and advise.

All these indicators will contribute to the formation of equilibrium prices, and to rate the different countries in terms of agricultural and environmental strategies. For that purpose, the agency consists of a committee of international experts and will be consolidated by a group of the wise men consisting of personalities of international renowned (former heads of state, "great consciences" ...). These committees of experts will meet regularly to define the levels of these indicators, advise and note the various concerned actors (regions, countries, companies). A bad grade will mean that an actor does not respect certain rules enacted and recognized by all. On the contrary, a good grade will reveal that the strategy led by this actor respects all the promulgated rules and works for the improvement of the collective well-being. Naturally, between both extremes, we shall find all the possible graduations.

And, as the world in which we live is characterized by an increasing interconnection of markets, the information thus emitted will have a fundamental role, their impact on the economic and social and strategic decisions becoming more and more important. It is this set evaluation and rating that makes the agency a real tool of regulation, a permanent source of information to better supervise international negotiations, and a tool to raise awareness among authorities and public on the dangers and the drifts of agricultural markets.

The principles of governance, third pillar of this global agricultural governance, constitute a first approach of what could be the world organization of production. They include two types of principles: general principles, which are organized around the definition of equilibrium prices by farming sector; principles of organization by farming sector, which include the main producing countries, but also ensure a representation of consuming countries.

Let us imagine that some developed countries totally remove their border protections; let us imagine that the producers are supported only by aids unrelated to production. If world prices were to fall durably, most parts of the developed countries would end up with very fallow areas: all the farms, including the biggest, would be affected, because they suffer, like the small ones, from productivity gaps with the best of the globe.

And these countries would not be able to ensure their food safety anymore. Their agribusiness model would witness a terrible setback, while in a very short time they have reached a level of development which allows them to function on their own. Attacked from the outside, even at the regional level, because we blame them for their budgetary costs: it is to forget that the scope of agribusiness has grown and that it will continue to grow at a constant budget.

It is necessary to remember that this development was not made for agribusiness, even if, by force of circumstances, it concerned producers. Let us return to the postwar years. The big regionalization do not exist and the countries that will eventually constitute them have to recover. They are in a pathetic state, both on the industrial and the agricultural plan. Let us remember that the bread has been rationed in some of these countries. The urgency was to reconstruct the industry: agribusiness was controlled to supply these countries with food, while managing a transfer and a mutation of the rural population toward cities. To achieve this, the policymakers chose to transfer to the regional level the need of a protectionist strategy to stimulate the agro-production to do so that a successful agribusiness emerges.

Building agribusiness in these countries was a condition for a strong industrial power. Nevertheless, the situation was not easy: on one hand a massive use of imports is absolutely necessary; on the other hand, these same imports compete with the local production and prevent any development process. Any resemblance with the real situation of a developing country today would be fortuitous...

These countries are going to resort to a temporary protectionism. With the levy system, they will be able to permanently adjust the protection of borders. The regional agricultural markets in these cases will run away from the global fluctuations which, otherwise, would have prevented them from existing.

These markets are regulated by the levies, by the prices guaranteed inside and by the refunds used for exports: the foreign trade performed exercised a regulatory function. So that each remembers the pace of progress, let us call back that the first regional organizations of market came into effect only after the Marshall plan. And all these assemblies were already inspired by the American model: free market inside and conquest of the planet outside.

In the negotiations for the construction of these regional agricultural markets, the United States accepted the mechanism of the levy on the condition that the Europeans give up all the tariffs on oilseeds, then on maize grains during the Kennedy round. So, in return for the levy, countries in the list depended on the United States for the animal food, which will be made from the American sectors of soya and corn. Let us not forget: it is still the case today in majority. For oilseeds, it is through a system of subsidizing sales at loss (the deficiency payments) that the Americans support their production, in cruise mode. Industrialized countries in their majority will copy this system, while it was a question of starting this culture.

Since all the production is helped, this policy is expensive for these countries. With the increase of motorization, the whole was quickly a success marked by the disappearance of the herd of horses (the main source of energy for agribusiness), the increase of the number of dairy cows and the yield per animal which will lead to the dairy surpluses, the replacement of oat sole intended for horses by corn soles for dairy cows and appearance of cereal surpluses years later.

All this course was marked by serious pitfalls. The system was made to work with stable currencies between them. If currencies began diverging, it would also be the divergence of the system. However, in front of successive devaluations, the decision makers decide not to apply this system to production. They succeed, mostly by the invention of the monetary compensatory amounts. Compensatory amounts are invented ... in cases of monetary revaluation. The budgetary cost of these monetary disorders was important. A single currency, in these cases would have avoided these unfortunate consequences.

Each country will have different attitudes according to their interests and convictions. By construction, some were advantaged on their agricultural plan, what was the "coin currency" for the industrial development of others. But they will quickly understand that, to decrease the relative cost of their financing, they had only to develop their own agribusiness, which amplified the success of agribusiness in these countries. Conversely, other countries still, whose interests are somewhere else than in agribusiness for a long time, are not going to follow this way.

In so doing, they will increase their part of relative financing by adopting a purely financial attitude. That is because the more agribusiness produced, the more it cost in terms of budgets. Even schemes such as the tax of coresponsibility failed to slow down the system: agribusiness was in a way a victim of its success. A serious financial plan was needed. It resulted from it financial quotas by production: for example, for oilseeds, there was a guaranteed maximum quantity. Then, by being inspired by the American farm bill, which argues about multiannual plans, budget stabilizers appeared.

Finally, it was necessary "hit the rock" and to restrict the production by quotas. The implementation of dairy quotas was for most countries, a strategy that allowed in ten years, the total of milk producers to be reduced by 60 percent. The "social" character of the dairy production disappeared then, leaving in most cases an economic sector which agricultural and processing companies have grown and concentrated. In the vegetable sector, it was the introduction of fallow. Besides benefits on the reduction of production and on the rest of soils, this policy made it possible to start the crops intended for biofuels. This is a summary reminder, the purpose being simply to show that it is still possible to catch up the ratings, which are anyway better than shortages.

This "is not so simple," we must deal with a living system, thus, complex and with many chain reactions. So, as the stocks of milk disappeared, stocks of meat appeared: dairy cows, indeed, are also meat. The needs fodder surfaces decreasing, they were given to cereals ... for which we were inspired by the American set aside, which is a compulsory freeze. Let us point out a very important difference between the main developed countries and the United States.

In other industrial nations, it is very difficult for a farmer to leave an uncultivated land, which is not a problem for an American farmer. The design of the space is radically different: They have room (for production on one hand, and for the recreational on the other hand), while in other countries, food and landscapes must be obtained in the same place.

What changes the world geographical configuration since the Second World War? The majority of countries will have developed a very important agricultural potential, while their budgets will have been contained and the surpluses controlled. The increase of spending will have been followed by an increase of production. Then the spending will have altogether stabilized.

Throughout these years, the various countries strengthened the measures in favor of the environment; the various strategic reforms recognized the multifunctional character of agribusiness by distinguishing a "rural development" component, and by introducing the notions of "modulation" and "ecoconditionality" into their global approach. Modulation consists in transferring helps between pillars for the benefit of the rural development. And to receive all the aids, the producers must necessarily comply with the environmental guidelines (nitrates, phytosanitary), have maintained the permanent pastures (ecosystems having positive effects on water, grounds and biodiversity), and to have maintained lands according to the good agricultural and environmental conditions.

It is likely that these are instruments that will help in the future to guide agricultural strategies, "without a loose purse." To this essential environmental concern, it will be necessary to add the reduction in the levels of support to get closer to requirements of the international institutions and transform the support system "for the product" into a support system, "for the producer." The logic of the decoupling of the various aids by product was pushed to replace these "myriads" of aids by the unique aid of certain continents. During all these years, agribusiness was questioned during events that worried the consumer. We will come back to it. But we can already mention the "hormone calf," the "mad cow," the "chicken with dioxin," the "genetically modified organisms (GMO)"...

Since a quarter of century, in industrialized countries, the gap widens between producers and the rest of the populations: consumers and citizens. The link is broken, the time is over when everyone had a family member and a close friend in agribusiness. And as this break becomes obvious, it becomes simultaneously obvious that agribusiness will not be made without the consumers-citizens!

The food safety becomes a claiming, while agribusiness and agro-production have never been that safe. Quality becomes a leitmotif and quantity is not a concern anymore. The terroir takes a new importance, while the distant exchanges multiply. The environmental protection is from now on a major concern, while the economic incomprehension is growing — and the disapproval — when addressing the question of farm subsidies.

It is more than necessary to make the consumer populations rediscover agribusiness, because agribusiness will not decide without them anymore. Agribusiness? The agribusiness models of the world, their development and the great agricultural adventure of the countries around the world.

CHAPTER 4

THE AGRIBUSINESS MODEL

Understanding that today we are in a global-finite ecosystem in the many interactions, we try to see how the demographic, natural, and organizational constraints previously discussed draw "agribusiness models" by the year 2050. Let us detect the global drivers and let us put agribusiness — or the agribusiness models — back in this group. By the example of a cooperative group, let us understand capacities and limits of producers to organize themselves and let us see how certain large companies, partners of producers design a sustainable agribusiness.

For the next years, the evolution of the demographic mechanisms is relatively fixed, as we saw it. The natural processes (climate, resources) are more difficult to identify and organizational modifications of various sizes can be imagined. But the prospecting exercise must be undertaken to imagine that the productive efforts by region will have to be in order to meet the need of vital. Is South America going to become the main supplier of agricultural raw materials? Is the United States going to remain competitive? Will the big exporting countries with an extensive agribusiness conquer the Asian markets? What will become the industrial powers, bordered by countries with a significant agricultural potential such as Ukraine or Russia? Will the migrations of population change the situation? And the rising urbanization? Will climate change reduce the available areas of certain countries? Do deforestation and the degradation of the natural productivity of certain ecosystems (soil erosion, loss of biodiversity, greenhouse gases permanently reduce the productive capacities? Is the choice of agricultural technologies (agricultural revolution, "green revolution," reasoned agribusiness, "double green revolution") relevant? Are not the yields going to cap?

The equation to solve is not simple. However, an approach by successive scenarios was tried. The first scenario extends the historical trend: countries seek to be self-sufficient in agro-production, import from their closest neighbors or major global exporters. They first increase their cultivated areas rather than their yields, except those who successfully started a "green revolution." Naturally, all the countries do not reach that point and the difficulties are contained by strong public authorities: this scenario is called Order from Strength in the Millennium Ecosystem Assessment synthesis report. Broadly speaking, Asia, North Africa, and the Middle East must matter; sub-Saharan Africa would reach at best the food self-sufficiency; South America (but also Australia and North America) would export toward Asia.

The second scenario relies on a growth of trade. China mainly import from Brazil and Argentina, which massively use GMO, corn, and soya to feed their poultry. Brazil accelerates the deforestation of the Amazonia. China, North Africa, and the Middle East use obviously their surfaces and their resources at the maximum. South America triples its cultivated surfaces, realizes today all the considered irrigation programs, and increases its yields. Africa remains isolated and uses its own resources. Russia, Ukraine, and Kazakhstan export cereal. This scenario seems satisfactory, but it is very basic as it cuts the world in six zones only, supposedly homogeneous, which is not realistic. The expected increases of yield of the "green revolution" in Asia is not sufficient, because we already start from a high level. Irrigation is supposed to develop at the maximum and we do not take into account the deterioration of the environment. Also, South America, which should increase its yields by 50 percent, is heterogeneous. Yet, if the climate of Brazil is equatorial, that of the Argentina is relatively dry and cold. Furthermore, we suppose that immense pastures are conquered on the forest: the environmental risks are important and if the expected increases of yield are not met, it is necessary to rely on an even bigger deforestation.

The study shows that we stumble on the problem of yields, if we do not change the agricultural practices, and this after having tried to balance many factors: the migrations of agricultural populations, urbanization, and the disappearance of surfaces due to the rising oceans level (Bangladesh, Mekong, Burma, and Java). Besides, the calculations were made by supposing that the developing countries would all have a food system that has reached a level of diversification (relationship between meat and vegetables) close to that of Mexico a decade ago. It involves very uneven modifications of the relationship between meat/vegetables, and consequently increases of very variable vegetable productions depending on countries: 36 percent for China, 50 percent for India, 65 percent for Indonesia, 81 percent for Vietnam, 124 percent for Bangladesh; 13 percent for Egypt, 22 percent for Morocco, 30–50 percent for the poor countries of South America, 60–120 percent for the West African countries, from 60 to 125 percent in East Africa, from 80 to 140 percent for the countries of Central Africa... Who should give up the meat-based diversification...?

Without changing the agricultural technology practiced today, is it possible to double the production in Asia, while the yields have already doubled in thirty years? To also double it in Latin America? To multiply it by five in sub-Saharan Africa? And it should be multiplied by 2.5 in North Africa and in the Middle East, which is impossible! Is it realistic to go farther in the "green revolution" (already disputed for its negative effects)? What can bring the agribusiness of precision? And what to expect from the reasoned agribusiness?

Multiple technical aspects were addressed: fertility of grounds, water, purge, genetics of plants, space and light, pollination... Because the concern is well that of the sustainability of agribusiness. That of the viability of ecosystems, that is their resistance to "shocks" and their ability to continue. Step by step, the conviction is that both intensive and ecological solutions must be found. According to agronomists, various cases of ecologically viable, productive, and very productive ecosystems already exist in various ecological parts of the world. Inspired by this, they started again their scenarios.

The third scenario proposes "a double green revolution" with few exchanges between big regions. Concretely, we reduce the use of chemical fertilizers, herbicides, and insecticides. We use natural resources as much as possible: the biomass as the source of fertility, irrigation, natural pesticides. This scenario is based on likely yield assumption stemming from the current experiment. It corresponds to the adapting mosaic scenario of the Millennium Ecosystem Assessment; the assumption is that the world must considerably reduce international exchanges (it can be the case if the costs of transport depending on to the energy cost are very high) and that companies should individually find the technological solutions to their problems. But the use of an ecological technology would exist only in the case of countries or regions not having any other opportunity than to rely on natural resources.

In this case, Asia remains in deficit, as well as North Africa and the Middle East. Sub-Saharan Africa remains isolated, but increases its yields by 40 percent in fifty years, and multiplies cultivated areas by 2.6. Then Latin America could get out of increasing its cultivated areas. All in all, we observe once again that, even with the "double green revolution" technology, the food self-sufficiency in Asia, North Africa, and the Middle East is impossible.

The fourth scenario tests the "double green revolution" and the balance by international exchanges. Sub-Saharan Africa remains in the same conditions; it could increase its yields even more and consider being an exporter. The deficit of Asia, North Africa, and the Middle East is compensated by Brazil and Argentina, but also by Russia, Ukraine, and Kazakhstan. This scenario is a reminiscent of the Techno garden scenario of the Millennium Ecosystem Assessment, which associates a controlled international liberalization with new technologies, but without specifying that these would be about technologies with an ecological basis.

By making an analysis of sensibility on the yield assumptions, the study indicates that we can consider that the "double green revolution" is able to feed the whole world in the next years. However, it is without considering the cultivable areas necessary for biofuels. To cover all of the deficit in biofuels of industrial countries, Latin America and Africa would to have to dedicate almost all of their territory to energy production with high yields, which is not possible.

All in all, reducing the poverty and implementing the fourth scenario requires not only public strategies on land tax, the spread of techniques, and credit but also policies to eliminate the drop of agricultural prices for the poor producers as well as the instability of the prices: to maintain farming communities in situations of poverty, is to deprive the society in general of growth and development abilities.

We know it today, the short-term objectives of the reduction of poverty with will not be reached. Thus, the problem should be immediately reassessed. And from the agricultural point of view, the pursuit of the current trends should be stopped (scenario 1), otherwise the humanity risks to degrade the ecosystems by going beyond their capacities of resilience. The risk of not renewal of the potential of production is particularly visible in Asia, in North Africa and in the Middle East. It is also obvious for many countries; the food safety can no longer be achieved by the only autonomy: it is an obligation to reason with trade. And to think simultaneously at the global and local level about of the conditions in which the agricultural raw materials will be produced. Doubling the agro-production at the world level is certainly possible within a few years, but only if we do not go beyond the viability of each of the local ecosystems. For that reason, countries like Brazil or Argentina cannot be for the sole purpose of liberalizing trade: they must, for themselves as for the whole world, avoid a "mining" agricultural exploitation of their country. Also, China or Egypt should not to resist the import, at the risk of crossing the limits of the ecological no return.

Generally speaking, it is necessary to find the means to avoid that certain countries practice an "ecological dumping" by exporting at a low price their agricultural raw materials and by destroying their resources. Is it understandable, symmetrically, that other countries that have the means, protect their ecological basis at higher costs, while in the next years, all agricultures must be mobilized and that they will have all to make considerable progress by this date? Our world is a "finite" ecosystem. The regulation cannot only be made by markets. It is necessary to think of agribusiness differently: the international institutions are necessary, but not sufficient. The agricultural strategies are far from being eliminated by globalization.

We shall not return in detail on the nature of the strategies led by the United States and the industrial countries. Let us only recall that they "succeeded" and that the surpluses and the very important costs led the various blocks to include the farming sector in the negotiations on international trade. We shall not return either on the reforms, but it is necessary to recall some recent evolutions of the agricultural strategy in the United States. In the fair act, they introduced the reduction in public grants and the abolition of the crop rotation control systems to increase the role of the market, which worked as long as the prices of the big cultures remained high. During the campaigns that followed, they restored the reached levels of public supports to compensate for price reductions, and the valid agricultural guidance law for six campaigns remained online. All the governments that have the means intervene and the most developed agricultural strategies meet in the United States, in the countries with a zero growth, in Switzerland, in Norway, in Iceland and in Japan.

In Brazil — whose considerable potential and the advance was identified in the field of biofuels — two departments in charge of the production are found: one for the extensive agriculture and another one for the small exploitations (considering the small influence of importing producers, certain European countries considered the abolition of their department). And Brazil knows how to use international authorities, as it successfully attacked the United States and the countries with a zero growth to the WTO on cotton and sugar. Its alliance with the Argentina is clearer; those it tries to establish with China and India in G 20 seem less solid.

Who is going to feed the world in transformation? Demographic pressure + not stretchable arable surface + limited water resources + environmental requirements + rural/urban imbalances = changing countries are not meant to be agricultural powers directly in competition with the current powers.

India is the country where the "green revolution" triumphed: It will be impossible for it, however, to keep supporting massively its inputs by subsidies. It is a "full" rural world, with a very significant constraint on the earth and on the water, and a "devastation" of the natural environment. This country became the first global producer of milk; it is also the first importer of plant oil (from Malaysia). Considering the multiple constraints (religious taboos on the consumption of pork and beef), but also innovations introduced following the "green revolution" and the use of the biotechnologies (GMO, patents taken by the United States with Indian researchers), certain observers indicate that the future agribusiness is invented in India. But it will be observed as regards to the questions of industrial property, input subsidy, or social and environmental conditions of production. Also, India is a founder of GATT and that Russia — whose agricultural potential of was already mentioned.

Finally, the big agricultural exporting countries, such as Australia, Canada, or New Zealand, as well as all the least developed countries, have a commercial importance that remains limited today. Producers of certain countries "live" on "semisubsistence" farms, bordering large farms from five hundred to two thousand hectares on average.

But it is rather the implementation of the last reforms that risks to change the evolution of agribusiness. As already mentioned, certain countries chose to remain important producers — "decoupling" at the most of the direct aids and reducing as much as possible the fallout, especially in regions with a lower agronomic potential. With the data from the agricultural accounting information networks, simulations were realized. They reveal that the surface of the big cultures would move back almost everywhere, except in the zones where cereal, oleaginous plants, and proteaginous are dominant and in certain countries, marked by the presence of the durum wheat. Conversely, the fodder sole would increase, especially in mixed zones, while the herbivore livestock would decline in the areas of big cultures: thus, it is the return to the specialization that takes shape worldwide.

We distinguish the following types of exploitations: intensive and competitive at the international level, specialized in the big cultures or in the dairy production, subjected to the environmental protection by means of conditionality and, for some of them, producers of raw materials for the nonfood industry (bioenergy, biomaterials); less intensive and producing farm products at the same time (bovine and ovine meats, milk) and of natural and landscaped heritage; productive of farm products (local specialities protected designations of origin) and/or of environmental services; producers, especially in touristic place, could frequently be multiskilled; specialized in aboveground productions (pork, poultry meat, also dependent on their own cycle of production) or in the vegetable, fruit, or wine production. In the case of permanent cultures, the territorial dimension and the landscape impact must be also be highlighted.

It is the result from a simulation, but this one does not take into account the behavior of the other actors of the sectors. The short supply chains will put producers in direct contact of with consumers (we will try another evaluation further). Whereas, the agricultural exporting potential will be manifested in sectors, especially by their part of agro-production, when it exists. It will be necessary to underline the necessity of pursuing — or to resume — the effort of competitiveness on a determined number of basic products (wheat, barley, sugar, colza), at the same time toward the imports of the "rest of the world." This effort will also be fruitful toward the production of biofuels and biomaterials; The opportunity to turn, at the level of the food industries, to transform products with a high added value, both on the regional and international markets, in the animal sectors as well as in the vegetable sector, and by diversifying the structure of export; the opportunity to look for a bigger adaptability in the export in the wine and spirits sector.

However, these indicator lines do not define a strategy nor the ambition for the real actors, producers in the first place. We talk about them as "peasant discomfort" and demonstrations seem to reveal to some a situation of despair. They do not have any more successors: it is not only the end of farmers, but it is also the end of the sons of farmers. Their economic situation becomes precarious: for a base of a hundred in a few years ago the income by assets in real terms is only 86.5. The agricultural world hesitates between anxieties and a "fed up" today. While their diversity is a strength, the producers remain obsessed by the peasant unity. They communicate on the way of "we are all farmers" and, at the same time, they demanded laws to make their status of business managers recognized. Their approach around the definition of their profession is schizophrenic, and this verbal schizophrenia maintains the discomfort. They do not know which agribusiness they wish, and the rest of society either. Their inability to name themselves is echoed in the society's inability what agribusiness might be. The agricultural profession is not disqualified and it cannot be defined. Only by accepting the individualities that come to light, will this profession build a real collective project.

The first job by the agribusiness has to remain that of the production of foodstuffs, but some want to convert the agricultural world to the nonfood productions; the farmers explore the markets of the future, the green tourism, the decorative and perfume plants, linen and hemp, pets, biofuels and biomaterials, green chemistry.... At the same time, all these jolts are transforming the farmers into professionals of agribusiness: their support is essential as well as the "advice," so that they can succeed in a more autonomous agribusiness.

The impression is that, in fact, not only he has grounds there is no real need to talk about a unitary peasantry that no longer exists, but that also, it is no longer possible to really talk about agriculture. If there are professionals of agribusiness, they should rather be compared to medical professionals: in number, specialities, professionalism, and commitment. From then on, several modalities of agribusiness could coexist in the world. These modalities were explored, and it would be really interesting to revisit the analysis in the light of the changes that occurred: WTO negotiations, reforms, agricultural guidance law... Within the framework of the present chapter, we shall be content to summarize the characteristics of the four scenarios, spotting key players and sketching the likely impacts according to seven types of agricultural regions in developed countries.

The four scenarios are scenario 1, an agribusiness centered on agriculture, where agricultural entrepreneurs, agricultural lobbies, and public authorities are key players; scenario 2, an agribusiness centered on industry, where firms, industry, mass-market retailing, and subcontracting producers are key players; scenario 3, un identity agribusiness, where agricultural entrepreneurs and transformers are key players, supervised by public authorities; scenario 4, a rural agribusiness, where key players are regions and rural entrepreneurs.

Industrialized countries will be in differentiated situations, according to their potential, the importance of the past and the energy of men. The plains of extensive culture, that is, approximately 15 percent of areas would be very favored in the scenario 1. The scenario 4 does not suit on them.

The farmland intensive breeding would be very concerned by the scenarios 1 and 2. They are already very committed in the industrial order. The relocation of the production units of pork and poultry is already at work; it could also be the milk production. These countries could be valued within the scenario 4.

The zones of agribusiness specialized intensive have a well-asserted fame and their productions depend few on agricultural strategies. The impact of the scenarios 2 and 3 would be very favorable to them.

The agricultural territories with low potentialities and a little attractive are already victims of the abandonment of farmland. These zones with low densities were only little concerned by the industrial scenario; the scenario 4 would be the most favorable.

The intermediate agricultural regions would be favored by a preservation of agricultural strategies, whereas the scenario 3 does not find many fulcrums there. The scenarios 2 and 4 would be favorable.

Rural areas with strong tourist valuation arrange of one agribusiness, which already practices the direct selling, the welcome, and the restoration. They are characterized by a strong presence of second homes. These territories are favorable to the scenario 4, that of the agribusiness functional. The scenarios 1 and 2 would not be favorable to them.

The scenarios "adaptation of the agricultural strategies" and "order industrialist" concern little outlying suburbs and coasts (that is, 10 percent of spaces in the world). The scenario 3 would be favorable to them and the very favorable scenario 4.

The intermediate agricultural regions would be favored by a preservation of agricultural strategies, whereas the scenario 3 does not find many supports there. The scenarios 2 and 4 would be favorable.

Rural areas with strong tourist valuation have an agribusiness that already practices direct sales, receptions and catering. They are characterized by a strong presence of second homes. These territories are favorable to the scenario 4, that of the agribusiness functional. The scenarios 1 and 2 would not be favorable to them.

The scenarios "adaptation of agricultural strategies" and "industrial order" do not concern outlying and littoral suburbs very much, that is, 10 percent of the global areas). The scenario 3 would be favorable to them and the scenario 4 very favorable.

We do not frankly go toward a dual agribusiness. If certain countries want to remain agricultural powers, they must experience a new "green revolution." There are two ways for farmers: the quality niche or the hunt for yields. And there will be no room for everybody. The expansion probably wants to indicate by there that in every case, producers of these countries "are condemned" to excellence. There are no more farmers and certain countries will have to train the producers who will be lacking by looking for new entrepreneurs in the whole of society.

We suggested that the world would need all of its producers, and that certain countries must be extremely careful if they want to be able to use the agricultural assets they built, in particular by promoting in the world a strong agricultural crop. But what happens today? It is as if no one can restore a strong "sense" for the world to start an ambitious new construction on the basis of a demanding analysis of the strengths and the current agricultural weaknesses of their models. We have the impression of an opposition to progress: the WTO, the effective implementation of the agricultural reform, the elections, here and elsewhere... And in the meantime, no heckling in ranks! That the laws of agricultural orientation suit to the immediate desiderata and that they just give the necessary room for maneuver for the relief producers. So, these laws do not seem to give direction. They do not contain the "big design," probably because society is not conscious of what they want as agribusiness. However, they were adopted by decision makers.

But where is the guide? What do we want? We are "disorientated." Conscious of the perspectives that the growth of the world demography and the new stakes, in particular environmental and sanitary, offer to the agricultural world and the agro-productions, to which the agribusiness is able to provide answers, industrialized countries give it a new boost as well as to the sector of agro-production for the next years. The various stakeholders will not fail to use the proposed openings; but the facts will lead them, one and the other, to meet the challenges with more vigor.

Nevertheless, let us take up the main objectives of these various standards:

1. Toward the agricultural company. It is about moving from the family exploitation to a real company. These rules modernize the status of farms and facilitate their transmission (creation of an agricultural fund and a transferable lease; fiscal and social measures encouraging the inflow of foreign capital and facilitating the progressive transmissions). They improve globally the working conditions and the social welfare of the producers (spouse status; facilitated vacation) and aim to develop wage employment;

2. Consolidate the income of producers and the "production." The different regulations give mission to the agronomic research the task to develop the nonfood valuations of farm products and have strong ambitions for the development of biofuels. In the various countries, these laws authorize the use of the pure vegetable oil for self-consumption and plan or allow their marketing as

agricultural fuel. They consider that the ban on the distribution of nonbiodegradable plastic disposable bags would be a strong sign of the will of public authorities to develop biomaterials to protect the environment.

Almost everywhere, they strengthen the interbranch organizations, in particular, to fight against the risks and the hazards, "by authorizing them to develop standard contracts between producers and buyers." So, they wish to give a new impetus to the global agricultural cooperation: in certain cases, they create structures responsible for the approval of all the agricultural cooperatives and encourage a dynamic management of the social capital and a better participation of the members. The generalization of crop insurance is envisaged in certain countries, as well as the acceleration of payments in case of agricultural disasters. Certain countries facilitate fiscally the functioning of a savings account intended to face hazards.

3. Meet the expectations of citizens and consumers. Structures of food sanitary safety, depending on the circumstance, assess the risks concerning phytosanitary products and fertilizers. The quality signs are gathered in three groups: they manage the signs of a superior quality, formerly, protected designations of origin and protected geographical indications, to the tradition or to an environmental quality; a particular labeling, concerns the developing mentions; the certification of product conformity to identify the specific characteristics of a product and to reproduce them throughout the production line and throughout the processing. The various standards support the biological production by the granting to farmers a tax credit and include in the rural leases, clauses to protect the environment.
4. Value all the territories. These regulations according to countries contain have policies to strengthen the protection of the marine agricultural area. Some make possible the creation of protected agricultural zones and systems of valuation of farmlands. The specificity of the agribusiness of mountains is strengthened in certain legislation and others recognize the contribution of the agroforestry sector to the reduction of greenhouse gas emissions. National forest

institutions, according to countries, will participate more in the development of the new market of the wood energy.

5. Modernize the institutional environment of agribusiness. Certain standards specify the notion of technical institutes that must pursue the improvement of the functioning of the network of farmers' associations. The management of the aids to agribusiness is simplified and the agricultural offices are grouped in three poles: breeding, extensive cultures, and specialized cultures. In certain countries, the authorities establish public services of the artificial insemination and interprofessional organizations of the genetic improvement of ruminants. No doubt that certain major questions, as the economic organization, will be resumed before long.

If we were able to give an idea on what was the agribusiness of the last years by describing a farm, it is not possible any more today, following all the evolutions we dealt with. We can nevertheless have a relatively precise idea of the agribusiness of a region of the world by describing a cooperative group: the externalized activities are still found at the regional level. But we shall not have a model of the "traditional farm." This is instructive and gives a concrete idea of the needs of the economic organization: it should constantly keep up.

In such a context, agricultural cooperative and of agro-productions groups should aim at developing their organizations and their missions on the scope of the cooperative. These should especially have the role of organizing of the production of the members, whose numbers quickly decreases: structural costs must be immediately adjusted, as well as the skills; the advice activities to the members become very "sharp," the members themselves often having a senior technician's level or having been themselves technicians of the cooperative; and the advice activities must be paid ... facing the competitors of the farmers' association technicians, financed by additional levies. So, the leaders of the various cooperatives, when they handle their management problems, would be ready to recommend that levied taxes on their own members are reduced (here is a concrete aspect of the life of agribusiness: all the producers contribute to farmers' associations, 90 percent of them at least are members of a cooperative).

Other role of parent companies is the one, directly or by the channel of "subholding companies," to carry the titles of their subsidiaries and participation forming the group cooperatives. So, the members of cooperatives will be present on seven sectors: cereal, milk, poultry, beef, pork, vegetables, and drinks (cider). These cooperatives will also have an activity of agro-supply (fertilizers, seeds, phytosanitary) and an agro-industrial activity (cattle food). They will have to create subsidiaries for fiscal reasons for their distribution activities "green point" (They will make their activities with more than 20 percent of customers who are not members of the cooperative, in particular in gardens and do-it-yourself) and the distribution activities of agricultural mechanization.

They will handle the direct valuation of crops grain. For milk, they will have a supply contract with the dairy Company. Except for the activity "egg packaging," for which they hold a minority interest, all other activities of valuation are often or should be the fact of subsidiaries grouped in companies: one for the flesh poultry, one for the processing of bovine meat and pork (it would be a company of capital only held by cooperatives), another one for the first range of vegetables and for the fourth range, a structure, finally, that transforms cider fruits.

We have just described agribusiness met on the perimeter of this cooperative (territorial company). Everybody can understand the difficulty there is to tell producers, whose company is territorially limited, that it is necessary to establish and to base companies in England, in Mexico, in Spain or in Tunisia to succeed in vegetables. And when we know that the cash flow of these companies is essentially generated by the activity of subsidiaries abroad, things are even less simple. Nevertheless, the whole would work and drain the rural economic life by its agricultural activities and its very developed network of numerous rural stores: the role of these groups in the town and country planning is obvious.

Let us add finally that the producers of vegetables are a very small minority of the members of the cooperative; everybody imagines then the importance — and the difficulty — of cooperative life so that these groups remain viable and coherent. These cooperative's board of directors will consist of members who are producers. They will be elected by the delegates during the annual general assembly for a renewable four-year term. The members of the board will represent the territorial regions or the sectors of animal and plant productions, which have representation structures: it is the regional and sectorial council that will oversee the follow-up of activities and the elaboration of the guidelines according to the annual budget and the three years plan. (...). The Council also leans on commissions. (...). It also intervenes, through the representatives, in the committees of control or boards of directors of the subsidiaries, which will make up the group.

This example could be infinitely detailed. Its history, begun with that of the first farmers' unions, is edifying: the trend of "selling to produce" won against the "production" trend. It is still much "centered on agriculture," even if the adventure introduced by certain very independent (producer-entrepreneurs), is put forward to highlight the cooperative success in the international agro-production. Also, not insignificant part of the members entered directly with a capital of these models of companies: this orientation illustrates well the will of the groups (several billion dollars of turnover) to consolidate their downstream activities, more than ever essential to reach markets and consumers.

Some lines of the annual report of these structures give indications to the orientations in place. We observe that the use of fertilizers keeps decreasing and that the agronomic practices and the follow-ups of cultures are more and more precise (use of Farm stars for the advice of the plot of land from satellite pictures); that the surfaces of corn decrease in parallel to the dairy intensification, which pulls the decrease of the dairy livestock; that surfaces of colza increase very significantly (these structures implement all the means to guide producers in the development of this culture promised to a bright future with biofuels); or that the logistic device from port facilities in various countries allows a direct delivery to the farmer (the network store helps to keep in touch with the producers with insufficient volumes).

Let us notice the launch of the use of the futures markets to allow the breeders who desire it, to set in the medium term the prices of the product. The market of milking robots of quickly evolves with the increases of size of the dairy livestock further to the restructurings of exploitations. The fiscal advantages lead producers to choose of the new rather than the used while the disappearance of the small exploitations strikes a very hard this second-hand market.

The complementarity of the ponds of production of fresh vegetables limit the effects of the climatic hazards and the fact that the Internet network is used to optimize the harvest of salads according to market needs and the responsibility of industrial facilities: all in all, certain brands consolidate their positions by putting forward an approach of sustainable development, whereas others, with turnovers of several million looks in the world, for the zones of growth on a more and more competitive market. Besides, the review of the contractual relations between the producers of orchards "low stalk" which was driven by certain subsidiaries on one hand and, on the other hand, the communication on other brands, allowed the global recovery of sectorial performances.

The report of these structures was marked by very lively tensions within the dairy interprofession before reaching an agreement in certain cases on the terms of payment of the price of the milk. (...). The price of the milk, until then unique, better had to consider the situation of markets and it is what was decided in the new system of the recommendation of the price of the milk with the mechanism of flexibility allowing to adapt the price of the milk (paid to the producer) to the product mix of every (processing) company. With the productivity gains of the dairy production, the essential cows to supply the processing tools are not numerous enough anymore, while the purchases of the households are progressing despite the prices and before the avian crisis. The majority of these companies encourage the production of young cattle, the only alternative, to the structural decrease of the offer of animals "of reform" and at the demand of the market. The evolution of the economic environment, which results from current reforms, leads us to apprehend this production in new conditions around three major axes: Produce a dairy type of young bovine, having a sufficient stock and finally improve the technical and economic performances in breeding.

For its part, the very sophisticated and very professional management of the poultry branch in certain countries has made it possible to obtain results in contrast with the whole industry. This performance is due to the positioning in fresh products and elaborated products, with a steady development in the various segments of the distribution (closer to the strategy of vegetables: a tense flow pulled by the consumer of fresh/live products/services — cut poultry, peeled and mixed salad — cold logistics). On the other hand, the egg consumption activity suffered, except in the label. For embryonated eggs, intended for vaccination against influenza, the choice has been to reduce the activity because of the unpredictability of production, sanitary in particular, and consequently of management of risks which is difficult to ensure.

The portrait of this polyvalent cooperative could be completed by those of many others, which would show that cooperatives are an instrument of organization of production (atomized among very many producers) extremely valuable. However, some of them are specialized in the common use of factors of production, such as cooperatives for the use of agricultural equipment — and we know the importance of motorization in productivity gains — or cooperatives. Artificial insemination — and we know they're determining role in the spread of animal genetics. In total, the millions of cooperatives in the world and their subsidiaries, that is millions of wage earners mainly in rural areas, distribute their turnover between cereals (26 percent) and meat (21 percent), milk (20 percent), wine-growing (7 percent, with very many very old cooperatives), animal feed (7 percent), distribution and services (6 percent), fruits and vegetables (5 percent), sugar (3 percent), and other activities (5 percent). While the collection function accounts for just over half of total activity, industrial processing accounts for more than a quarter. In the latter field, the market share of cooperatives is 80 percent for cider, 75 percent for table wine, 60 percent for animal feed and sugar, almost half in pork, 4 percent in maize and malt, and one third or more in quality wines, the dairy or beef industry, milling, and champagne.

We have understood the essential and multiple roles of these companies in the organization of producers. It remains fundamental, even when they reach important sizes and become international. They cannot escape agribusiness or territory, even if they launch pseudopodia in agro-production and abroad. And while they are not immune to the restructuring and concentration of the agro-production sector, they are, in essence, linked to the act of producing agricultural materials. There is no doubt that they will have a huge role to play in the sustainability of the production activity, by surely taking part in the establishment of young people (they are a school for economic training and responsibilities of young people) and ensuring sustainable agribusiness. Private industries, which do not have this "organic" link with agro-production, multiply actions, under the pressure of consumers in particular, to ensure an explicit link with this vital activity: agribusiness.

Danone, Nestlé, and Unilever are the founders of the sustainable agriculture initiative platform: a platform to promote development and communicate on sustainable production, involving all stakeholders in the food chain. We must be aware of these global movements: producers attached to a territory that, through their cooperatives, will reach a final consumer, elsewhere in the world; multinational industries, pressed by consumers to ensure a vital link to their food that comes from an agriculture necessarily very localized.

The challenge of today is to break the link between the economic growth and its negative impact on the environment: there are clear limits in the capacity of the earth. Yet, if the food is essential in life, how many consumers know how it was cultivated, transformed, transported, and distributed? So that all in the world can meet these vital needs without compromising the future generations, what should require from the agribusiness system? Agribusiness and the producers, having been strongly marked by the agricultural strategies of the developed countries, will they be led in the future by the industrialists of transformation? Who would look in the sustainable agribusiness only for a simple selling point? That a subsystem enslaved of the food system?

Think of agribusiness differently. Think of the agricultural productions otherwise. With the general concerns of the globe and the human world. With the sometimes very local concerns of the actors of transformation and distribution. While it became a complex system, cross-linked to infinity in which each of actors must be able to say which agribusiness he wants, at the risk of being without any strategy, without will, without mechanisms and without future.

CHAPTER 5

INDUSTRIES, DISTRIBUTION, LOGISTIC

The agribusiness system no longer really has a center, or origin, as the "primary" nature of production might suggest. Rather, it reveals multiple sequences of companies of all sizes; the link with production is, however, an obligation, a must. We have just seen that agribusiness cooperatives are an impetus for agro-production and that, conversely, very large firms are concerned about the permanence of their link with production. In the first case, agribusiness is a "raison d'être"; not in the second, where it is, however, a sine qua non condition, as long as the object of the firm remains food (this point is not a detail: Danone is the result of successive transformations of BSN, operators in the glass, whose strategy was for a moment, from the container to the contents, from the glass to the beer, then to the agriculture production in general, which is not quite the case anymore today). In addition, companies that absolutely need agribusiness are very diverse in size and influence over their agricultural supplier, sometimes confined to the role of subcontractors (but cooperatives have agro-production subsidiary). We will explore this part of the agribusiness system in depth in this chapter.

We should also look at all the suppliers of agribusiness: manufacturers of fertilizers, phytosanitary, machinery, and equipment, suppliers of seeds or feeds who have provided themselves with agribusiness. Within the limited scope of this chapter, we chose not to go into details; this important question is, however, generally mentioned in the previous chapters, and it will also be later. Let's say, however, that the actors in this part of the agribusiness system are fully concerned by the development of production: they are innovators, in competition and their concentration is important; they risk seeing the demands of producers benefiting from agricultural strategies fall in volume and become more demanding in quality and precision, if the protections of these countries come down; they are obviously very interested in all the mechanisms that would favor the growth of other producers in the world for which they would become suppliers. Their impact is considerable and their responsibility sometimes sought by the final consumer. Their partners are essentially the actors of the agricultural distribution, first and foremost the cooperatives. Their "distance" to everyone, the ultimate consumer, is quite long; on the other hand, the distance of the final consumer to the food processing industry is shorter: only the food distributor separates them physically, because they are often in direct communication by the brands of manufacturers. Nevertheless, the question here is about traceability: what is in the food? Pesticide? genetically modified organism (GMO)? We will come back to it.

Whatever they are, food products are very fragmented: their actors are very numerous and small. In front of them, the agricultural model is made up of truly heterogeneous actors and the sector remains very fragmented. It is necessary to look closely at it, to avoid a bad appreciation of the links uniting those of these chains and these networks.

At the level of each region of the world, we have statistical information on the food industry and beverages. There are hundreds of thousands of companies, gathering millions of employees, for a turnover of several hundred billion dollars. "Micro" enterprises, with fewer than ten employees, account for 7 percent of the sector's turnover. They account for 16 percent of employment and 9 percent of the added value. They constitute three quarters (78 percent precisely) of the total number of enterprises in the sector.

"Small" firms, with ten to forty-nine employees, account for 15 percent of turnover and added value. They represent 17 percent of the companies in the sector.

The "average" companies, from 50 to 249 employees, account for 26 percent of turnover and 23 percent of added value. They represent "only" 4 percent of the total number of enterprises on average in developed countries. "Large" firms, or 1 percent of the total, are responsible for 52 percent of turnover and turnover. Fifty-three percent of added value, while they employ 39 percent of the workforce.

Although this sector is the most important of the economy of the rich countries (about 13–14 percent of the turnover, added value and employment), before that of the "automobile" and "chemistry" industries its growth is modest (we have seen that the populations of some countries have begun their demographic regression, which directly affects the volume of food consumption). They remain, however, exporters. Labor productivity is below average for all sectors. And we must judge that its profitability does not grow sufficiently. On the other hand, if gross margins remain above 20 percent for large firms, they are only slightly above 6 percent for medium firms, while they are of the order of 2.5 percent for the small ones. The average performance of the large ones, measured by the operating result, is around 7 percent, while that of the others is around 4 percent. We observe that investments are in slight decline, in some countries; they are growing elsewhere. Moreover, the sector, characterized by many brands, is significantly the object of counterfeits from Russia, Ukraine, the Dominican Republic, Nigeria, and Argentina...

The sector appears to be lagging in several European countries in terms of growth and labor productivity compared to countries such as Brazil, Australia, or Canada; at the same level as the United States in these terms, but better than them in added value. Export market shares are declining, led by Brazil, China, Australia, New Zealand, and other countries.

From this group, where small- and medium-sized enterprises (SMEs) seem to be weakened, transnational companies such as

Pernod-Ricard or Danone emerge. If they can seem huge, it must quickly put into perspective, because Danone, with a market capitalization of billions of dollars, is four times smaller than Nestlé, its competitor, which capitalizes five times more billions of dollars. To protect from predators, one of Danone's means is to grow by buying other companies; it becomes more difficult to acquire.

For the developed countries, the sector's turnover is 150 billion on average; the many thousands of employees are employed on average by 11,000 enterprises, artisanal and industrial; 3500 of them have more than twenty employees or, 70 percent on average of the enterprises have fewer than twenty employees; many of them belong to groups of more than 500 employees: about 200 groups per country and 130 foreign groups of 500 or more employees are present in the industrial fabric of agro-production in Western countries. While the sector remains the leading exporter in some countries, there is, however, a deterioration of the trade balance in these cases.

As these production companies are the main direct outlet for agribusiness professionals, it is essential to grasp the main challenges to imagine their influence on agro-production. Processors now know that their home market is "mature." This is the reality of the "wall of stomachs": the population is stagnating globally. But it changes. In particular, it is aging, which modifies the food needs. But consumers — as we will see later — are subject to constant changes resulting from lifestyles that have become extremely diverse and variable: the profession thus faces a global problem of innovation and research and development. It turns out that in these areas, the food industry is doing less effort than its colleagues in other industrial sectors and the traditional rich countries, less effort than their global competitors, this being particularly true of SMEs. In line with the relaunch of the sectorial strategy aimed at making these countries the most competitive "knowledge-based economies" in the world, the agribusiness sector is trying to make known its "vision." Not surprisingly, it indicates that we are moving from a market that was marked by agricultural supply to a market that now depends on the demands of the consumer. This is the fork to farm perspective:

consumer demands will govern the future needs of research and development (R & D).

The other way to produce growth is to export to fast-growing foreign markets. To achieve this, the costs must be competitive, which can only be achieved by having access to agricultural raw materials that meet very precise specifications (quality in particular) and be present in sufficient quantities at adequate prices. The profession wonders about the future ability of the primary sector in some industrial countries to adapt their agro-production: will the uses of agricultural products for nonfood purposes (biofuels and biomaterials) become scarcer and more expensive? Intended for making food? Should we not reactivate globally, for example, the procedures for importing agricultural raw materials at the world price and reexport them after manufacturing food products? In general, the profession is worried around the world about the outcome of several current cycles and bilateral agreements (Mediterranean zone, Asian, Latin American...), nontariff barriers, promotion to the export, the development of regional standards at the global level, etc.

In their quest for competitiveness, processors want the government to take measures that promote business and, in particular, reduce administrative procedures, while leaving the regulations in an efficient manner (customs, additives, new products, labeling, packaging, hygiene, waste, pollution...).

And they are worried about the extreme concentration of the distribution sector: the top five, control more than 90 percent of the distribution in Sweden, more than 60 percent in the Netherlands, more than 55 percent in France and England, more than 40 percent in Germany. They increase their bargaining power by purchasing regional power plants. And they are increasing the proportion of private-label products, while hard discount is gaining market share.

What will become of the food network? Will power not be able to focus on a relatively small number of large processors, and on a much smaller number of distributors? If so, what is the future role of SMEs and producers? Will SMEs not also focus? Some will find, on the contrary, advantage to remain artisanal? While a significant proportion of agricultural microenterprises will reach the size of some industrial SMEs? Is it so sure that we will stay in an almost unique fork to farm? Or will poles not be aggregated differently into business bouquets on the food web? Poles from which the creation of agricultural, food, nutritional, cultural, or natural value will be driven?

Are we not prisoners of ways of seeing that lead us necessarily to too little enthusiasm, if not to a real pessimism? For example, it is curious that investors are interested in a sector that seems so dull. And we believe it is useful, without claiming to make a complete picture of agro-production, to report some observed trends that show the vitality of food.

Matured markets, not much growth (but regular), demographic recession, reduction of margins, decrease of investments, the agribusiness sky seems indeed cloudy. But these clouds are in perpetual movement. The agro-production must innovate and focus. It is finally a sector with many new ideas and which, because of its fragmentation in several companies, benefits from many small entrepreneurs. It is exactly what investors are interested in. It is also necessary to understand that the interest is not due to the particular general and medium characteristics of the market but the particular characteristic of some operators. In reality, the winners are the well-informed operators and companies. Paradoxically, in a sector that seems so dull and so close, the economic intelligence, make the difference.

Some "nonrepresentative" examples provide information on what pleases investors. It cannot be avoided to criticize some groups, as the virtual OPA for instance, which triggered a while ago an "economic patriotism" movement. In those cases, the stock market price increases of 25.5 percent. In fact, those groups continued with their refocusing strategies by cessions that obviously interested other operators: so was the case of the sauces (Amoy in Japan, HP Foods in the United Kingdoms, Lea and Perrins in the United States), the water DS Water tanks, or the British biscuits.

Those groups are now focused on dairy products, water, and biscuits. Their main markets are in Chile, Tunisia, Thailand, Eastern Europe and China, which represent, 10 percent of the turnover (Franck Riboud notices that "moreover, Chinese people include the healthy benefits of dairy products."), while other regional markets guarantee 54 percent of their activities. But the American market also interest those giants, as it represents 10 percent of their income. On this market, yogurt — and precisely organic yogurt — that succeed with their subsidiaries: they often outpace the groups selling their brand... Yoplait (Walmart could extend its yogurt shelf of 1 m). And from this experience, these groups could create new brands of "organic" yogurt, to generate the same activity as Actimel or Activia (the new name of the "organic" yogurt, whose packaging shows that the ingredients were not so organic).

For those operable groups of which 86 percent of the capital is public, and in which there are no hardcore shareholders of which quarter of employees is Chinese, whose goals are to acquire SMEs to be present in at least eighty countries versus forty today, and on which market is global at 50 percent, the competitive advantage does not lie in their origins. The nationality of the executives does not really matter, but that of the directly active business operators do. It is also said that those groups are managed as SME: when you will come from an Anglo-Saxon company, the guidelines are not understandable, and those firms are not operable to anyone.

They can be young and small, but regular growth of 15 percent, international, on the stock market and very innovative. This is the case of certain firms, which became global leaders of plant extracts intended for the food and nutraceutical industry, there are listed on the stock market, and often raise millions of dollars to finance their targeted acquisition programs. Based on local technological poles where they have a production area, research laboratories, they are present almost everywhere in the world (in Morocco, in New Jersey and in California, and they have an office in Singapore), count hundreds of contributors, and make many millions of sales, with 90 percent from export.

The investment funds are the guide of many operations. On one hand, many SME leaders reach retirement age and desire to sell their business, on the other hand, many groups are hurried by shareholders to focus on the core of the business and sell the subsidiaries, as in some cases. These movements offer opportunities to experienced entrepreneurs who lack capital, to start again their activities, that is, when investment funds intervene, they cannot run only on the market averages. Thus, these funds seek high yields, around 20 percent aimed at offering too those who benefit from the funds a yield superior to that of competitors. As they do not systematically succeed, they should severely select their operations. Very few files are completed (about 2 percent). A deep analysis is made using experts and networks (economic intelligence), weeks are spent writing scenarios likely to bring out any kind of rupture to create value. Then "oversized" managers are sought to carry out operations subject to very "tense" legal, financial, and fiscal arrangements.

Horizon of reflection is of about ten years, so that by selling after about five years, the target may be attractive enough for a new entrepreneur: it must remain a potential to serve as a basis for a new scenario. And when the case is over, "the speed of execution is incredible": two hours of meeting a month with the manager who was chosen for his creativity and experience. The strategy has been defined; its responsibility is to implement it: it is obviously interested in its success.

Very important operations can be carried out and change the local landscape of a sector (in four years, VION has become number one in Germany in the most fragmented sector of pork slaughtering, starting from the Mikel group, which accounted for 5 percent of market shares, the ZTLO fund followed by buyback operations, notably Savin and Sudfleish, leading to a leadership position with 22 percent of market shares). Inducing competitors to do the same, the sector has become structured, with three companies now accounting for 45 percent of the market.

Some specialized operators have been formed and agricultural funds are active, but all the funds are attracted by agro-production:

those that have existed for a long time are the best ones to make good operations, because their knowledge of the sector is necessarily important; so, they have specialists. Unlike agricultural, they do not necessarily seek to specialize, because their behavior is primarily opportunistic, seeking above all, targets whose rate of return on investment will exceed 25 percent. But since they have been in this business for a long time, they have accumulated experience that gives them a decisive advantage.

There is not really a rule; the eye must be keen and able to distinguish sometimes very different value-creating strategies from the neighboring basic data. The bakery-pastry sector offers an example. There are local heavyweights, become bread leaders and have subsidiaries in other countries. But we can meet some companies that develop mainly through their efforts of industrial productivity, alongside other structures that, on the same field of departure, constitute commercial groups, using the franchise. And we can see dynamic groups developing, in the fast-growing sector of sandwiches or motorway food distribution. These structures will surely continue their concentration: advances in deferred manufacturing techniques will grow in one direction, while the stigmatization of the sector about obesity will lead to new proposals; the shortage of manpower will be offset by innovations coming from equipment manufacturers; the development of "bakery-pastry" shelves in supermarkets will continue, despite these changes, to maintain customer flows and traffic. This will certainly not discourage some firms to do the "high end."

Returning to certain groups, formerly more specialized in dry pasta, we could evoke the radical changes that have taken place in a few years... We could "go for a ride" in the section of elaborate fresh products (which we also find in automatic distribution or on motorways). Dairy products (ultra-fresh, cheese, cream, butter) are a pillar of agro-production, looking for growth. The elaborate fresh fruits and vegetables can be very attractive: they do not require heavy industrial investments, while the activity is characterized by zero, or even negative, working capital requirements. This is the universe of the fourth range, dynamic; the fifth range: "caterer," salads that develop in MDD and that innovate in recipes and packaging; "fresh soups," struggling to take off; or niches like "fresh purees." It is a world where potential buyouts/purchases are numerous: industrial leaders are there along with cooperatives and traders.

We could also mention seafood, whose consumption increases when the resource becomes scarce and whose organization is complex, involving many intermediaries.

We could detail the world of "healthy" ingredients, that of companies that have a myriad of small businesses on the planet and whose problems are not necessarily simple: Is the scientific basis of these "healthy" foods enough? Is the "health" argument not already overused? Are the answers to obesity or aging serious? Are clinical studies conclusive? The health claims exact? Can "future" pathologies such as cancer or osteoporosis lead to new foods?

Are "slimming" products, which are strongly growing, a real future? In any case, there is a permanent renewal of the offer that differs with the appearance of "male" products, "young" products and "senior" products. We are at the crossroads of agro-production, pharmacies, and cosmetics: an illusion? Competitive groups that have just founded joint subsidiaries.

Should we return on earth? Let's look at prepackaged waters (mineral waters, spring waters, purified waters): they are packaged in materials made from oil. Will the ecological pressure water + plastic/oil not lead to changes, while at the same time, there is a significant drop in sales prices, the first prices pulling the market?

Another aspect of the issue of agro-production is the fact that consumption has slowed down considerably in the industrial countries, putting at risk the profitability of supermarkets. In the beginning, Ford granted, for example, high wages so that the workers could buy the "Model T," result of a mass production allowing to reduce the prices. Today, Wal-Mart is charging low prices for customers by putting pressure on wages. Using the most powerful computing and logistics devices, it gets its supplies from China (if Wal-Mart was a country, it would rank as China's eighth largest trading partner, ahead of Russia and Great Britain), putting pressure on margins suppliers. Have we not entered a downward spiral of prices and purchasing power? Is the constant search for the lowest price not at the expense of employment? Operational managers of mass retailers are convinced that they create jobs, especially for the least qualified; but is there not "collateral damage" on employment in general, caused by large retailers? What would be the net balance?

This caricature has the merit of highlighting the questions that are emerging, on the impact of mass distribution on the repartition of value along the chains that connect producers to consumers, and in particular producers to consumers of food products, that is, "all of us," However, to perceive the future evolutions, it is essential to go back into the details; we will focus on distribution in the industrialized countries.

It should first be noted that, although most of the food goes through large-scale distribution, part of the food reaches the final consumer without going through mass distribution. The consumer goes to various formats: hypermarkets, supermarkets, convenience stores, and hard discounters. But they can also get their food through mail order, the "online grocery store," or automata; he can eat outside home, at the cafeteria, at the restaurant, or on motorways; and he can do his food shopping at gas stations. Conversely, mass distribution may not be food: this is the case for household appliances, furniture, sports goods, etc.

Also, although the food distribution is very concentrated, the combination of the different cases makes that the strategies of the groups or the brands can be very different. We will give an overview by trying to reveal some problems.

Today, retailers can be seen as an oligopoly: few sellers face a multitude of buyers-consumers who cannot know the prices well, given the number of references, the variety of conditions, etc. It can be seen as an oligopsony: they are a small number of buyers facing the large number of industrialists. Standards have tried to "administer" relationships between actors, inducing criticized behavior. The search for low prices after the war led some traders to "break the price." Producers, industrial and agricultural, tried to resist this move by refusing to sell to "price breakers," which became impossible as a result of regulations prohibiting the "refusal to sell." The small business has obviously suffered from this situation and many demonstrations have disturbed public order in some countries. Other standards have aimed to channel these movements, accompanying the modernization of distribution and helping small businesses.

Severe strategies have emerged, the creation of large areas generating the production of local taxes and jobs, on the one hand, and the increase of the brand activity that obtained the authorization to install. Corruption entered the system. At the same time, "broken prices" seemed welcome at a time when inflation was "galloping." Large-scale retailers shaped the landscape of cities and the countryside, while competition intensified: to maintain their activity in the short term, certain industrial and agricultural producers were forced to agree to sell below their cost price. In the medium and long term, this meant the disintegration of the industrial and rural fabric of certain countries, while, moreover, territorial development strategies were at work.

In other countries, the regulation introduced the prohibition of resale at a loss by the distributors and maintained the ban on the refusal of sales by the producers.

Also, standards imposed an authorization to open surfaces higher than 300 sq. m, which perfectly suited the hard discount for which this size is enough. Still others according to the countries will practice "back margins," a technique that consists in making the industrialist pay commercial operations, not always corresponding to real benefits from the distributor. Which distributor could brutally "deference" the supplier? It was necessary to reform again. The new economic regulations of these countries have prevented arbitrary "references." These standards aim to achieve a decrease of the price, in particular by systems that limit the back margins to an average of 20 percent of the purchase price.

The market shares of the retailers in the rich countries are divided by taking account of a world, which is made even more complex if one looks at the purchasing central in which the companies are grouped. We will give here only a few points of reference and some indications on the principal groups: some have as many workers as the army of their country; others belong to a hundred of family shareholders; some structures are independent cooperative groups (the generation of pioneers are now retired); the signs format of some companies (1200 sq. m) exempted them from the authorization of establishments and are also industrial in their agro-production, some structure, with a very small "starting setting," is today at the head of a fairly indebted group, some of which are, however, very profitable; a number of structures are groups of independent: "new traders," actually very involved in local life (sponsoring hundreds of thousands of associations) and favoring SMEs.

It is understandable that the strategies of these groups are remote:

1. In a difficult merger, some groups must monitor their share price in order to protect themselves from an OPA. They need to turn their profitability on their core business, the hypermarket, and take points on the competition. Highly concentrated in certain geographical areas, where they are perceived by the consumer as the least expensive brands, these firms extend their business to other worlds: first fuel, then jewellery, books, para pharmacy... Their members are in a patrimonial logic.
2. Certain firms have been the subject of a very "tense" financial construction and must satisfy the shareholders (profitability and deleveraging are its key words).
3. Others have a priority to revise the format of their hypermarkets, which are very large and less suitable for today's consumers.
4. Other groups have been in great trouble as a result of their international attempts with the acquisition of businesses, which they resold. They remain number one in the "supermarket" format.
5. Independent firms have concentrated all their efforts on local shops.

It will be quite interesting in this configuration, to observe how everyone has contributed to the objectives of the plausible regulation of lower prices in the different countries and to see the evolution in relation to agro-production. Households are spending a decreasing proportion of their income on food; distributors will therefore seek to capture flows from other nonfood sectors, without abandoning their pressure on the food industry and producers. Competition will certainly not weaken between brands: for food products, what new behaviors will we observe? Because price is not the only variable. To "move the game," what levers will be used, on the one hand, in the relationship between food producer and distributor and, on the other hand, in the relationship between food distributor and consumer? In what proportion is it conceivable that the relationship between food producer and end consumer goes through other circuits than those of large retailers?

The model to follow currently would be British. Indeed, in the world of agribusiness, Tesco is very profitable and is growing. It is powerful in England, where it controls the third of the food distribution. In search of growth drivers, it is becoming more and more international, particularly in fast-growing emerging countries, such as Taiwan, where it entered into competition with other groups, of course. These competitor distributors are also trading: Tesco sold its Taiwan operations, while some competitors gave up their stores in the Czech Republic and Slovakia. These operators are not at their first contacts: in its first steps abroad, Tesco bought very profitable supermarket chains. However, having failed to maintain this profitability, the English group resold them.

Tesco as well as the German hard discount stores are dynamic (they are not necessarily "pauperizing" models: there are close to quality products). Very demanding in terms of profitability, Tesco became "superprofessionalized," while the other firms have mostly worked on very specific local bases, especially in terms of payment time: honoring their suppliers by respecting the deadline, they benefit almost immediately revenue from consumers paying in cash. Some observers go so far as to say that distributors on average earn their money rather because of these particular financial arrangements than by properly exercising their trade of distributors: some firms would have fallen behind in the "fundamentals" of this trade.

Of course, Tesco is working on price and price transparency, while maintaining a record profitability: where most firms present a quarterly price basket, Tesco compares thousands of regularly updated prices. And it does not hesitate to mention that competitors like Wal-Mart or Sainsbury can offer lower prices because it has other arguments than prices. Its stores — opened 24 hours a day, 7 days a week — are irreproachable, the shelves always being filled. It must be noted that it has a real private label strategy (it develops its products and builds its ranges with manufacturers, rather than engaging in sometimes brutal sorting between suppliers). Its decisive competitive advantage lies in the way it manages its relationship with the customer (it has giant databases on products, but also on its customers).

Thanks to the club card, customers having one, benefit from a discount each quarter and receive offers targeted according to their buyer profile. In addition, it is the only distributor who has managed to develop a true cyber market. It is present on all formats of stores and invests in local areas while diversifying in nonfood, which allows it to further improve its relationship with the customer, by multiplying the services, financial services in particular. And to meet the global requirements of its customers, it communicates on its programs of use of renewable energies or on the construction of its new stores in recyclable materials.

Thus, thanks mainly to logistics (physical flow processing — size and distribution of stores and warehouses; collaborative management of stocks with suppliers — but also information — using powerful computer tools), it is necessary to expect not only a change in the relationship with customers, but also profound changes with local players in agro-production — craftsmen and manufacturers — and with producers, suppliers of unprocessed agricultural products. The information processing can be at the cause of a consequent modification of the relations of distribution with its customers and suppliers; it can also be the source of new behaviors between these same customers and suppliers and the restaurant sector.

The distribution of meal solutions is very popular. In developed countries, an average of one in three meals is taken out of home compared to one in twelve in developing countries. It can be argued that these are not the same meals; nevertheless, the practices of the actors influence one another and strongly change the landscape of the food "network,"

For example, the American Starbucks coffee shops are beginning to penetrate the city centers of all the rich countries, from which cafes are disappearing. Conversely, the "high-end" grocery stores that are characteristic of certain countries are taken as models by mass retailers around the world, and "big chefs" are asked by the agribusiness industry to develop "meal solutions." Bearing their signature.

Other known examples are McDonald's, or Pizza Hut, another franchise belonging to the American giant Yum Brands. Less well-known example, that of successful entrepreneurial structures: these collective catering companies (cafeterias, schools, hospitals...) have a turnover in billions of dollars. With their hundreds of thousands of employees, they are present in about eighty countries. In this business with particularly low margins, it is interesting to observe that these companies have chosen to ensure their growth by providing their customers with a whole range of services. In addition to catering, other "support" activities are offered: maintenance, security, receptions, standard, cleaning, mail, reprography, etc. While some new players have chosen to remain focused on their business and grow through external growth and internationalization.

We are certainly in mature markets. However, we can see how changes in consumer habits and the concentration of actors are powerful drivers for changing consumer-distributor or restaurant-industry-producer relationships. The example of certain structures, which were strongly destabilized during the mad cow crisis, shows how closely consumers and producers are in close relationship, despite what separates them. For obvious reasons of safety, but also because they must constantly improve their efficiency, all these fragmented actors are constantly on the lookout for technical innovations to increase transparency, fluidity and reliability; reduce labor, inventories and stock outs; to make order picking more efficient and increase customer service: barcodes are everywhere, and the integrated labels will significantly improve management performance.

The working methods are deeply affected. Restaurant owners are looking for innovations to make the job easier and to remedy the lack of staff. Manufacturers are reviewing their receipts and their organization of production to adapt their series to the new ranges, wholesalers and cash & carry, where the "trades of mouth" come to stock up. Agribusiness processors also have to adapt to the particular demands of automatic distribution. Take the example of Compass: in the fight against obesity (withdrawal of automatic machines in schools), this company has changed agribusiness industry portions of snacks (less than two one hundred calories, six grams of fat, two hundred milligrams of sodium, twenty grams of simple sugars). The industry is also transformed by adapting: we now talk about "extra catering."

Everything moves, decidedly, in this sector of the restaurant, which directly affects the consumer, the "eater." And the most modern development methods penetrate, like the "franchise." In its organization, their selection is essential: nine out of ten candidates are rejected. And, imitating the rule of one-third time in force in the circuit, the franchisees devote their energy to the network. Investors also believe that the key question is that of people: they no longer hesitate to invest in commercial catering alongside teams of experienced people who create, innovate and concentrate businesses. In this particularly complex system, many networks connect the farmer and the consumer.

And how far is the responsibility of the operators? They are anxious to understand their responsibility. Competition between operators forces each of them to go beyond the rules imposed in terms of safety, especially since some pesticides can come into direct contact with the consumer, as is the case in fruits and vegetables. For example, the trade union has developed a school of good professional practice. On the other hand, some sectors aim to destroy all unused crop protection products and recover packaging. Finally, the innovation — crucial in this sector where concentration has reduced the number of operators able to do research at four or five — is not only about molecules; it also involves designing decision support tools that make it possible to optimally use the right product, at the right dose and at the right time, depending on the disease.

The case of certain firms is also very interesting: the food they market comes from poorly processed agricultural products (vegetables, poultry). We do not know how to improve the quality of a material that arrives in a factory, we can only preserve it at best. The link between the farmer and the final consumer is therefore direct. The consequence is that the entire organization, from the agricultural producer (who is also a user of crop protection products) is "obsessed" by the "no crisis": in this perspective, traceability is conceived as a tool allowing the systematic removal of products in case a problem arises. Traceability has been used as a real tool in some cases to meet the information needs of the consumer: varieties, cultural practices, industrial processes ... The consumer perceives traceability as an "identity card," as a "policeman" and as an "attentive mother": "the identity card is the product's history; the gendarme concerns the control and the respect of the standards; and the attentive mother is concerned with the quality and the permanent way of improving the products."

Innovation and food safety are at the center of operators' concerns: to obtain balanced products (less salt), healthy and safe (no risk of listeria or salmonella), while limiting costs and selling prices to the consumer, some companies have resorted to consulting firms that have developed new manufacturing processes. But some companies have hesitated to file these patents (indeed, in agro-production, when filing a patent, it is often revealing a manufacturing secret to competition).

All these points are debating, obviously. What do we really know about the eco-toxicology of chemicals and their long-term effects? Have consumers really given themselves the means to communicate to food partners? There are consumer associations around the world who do not fail to stress that the issue of the cost of food cannot be separated from the question of the cost of health. Because what they pay less in the basket of the housewife, they pay it in addition, partly in their expenses of health. The day we come to establish in everyone's mind the connection between the two, we can move towards smarter strategies.

At what level should the public authorities intervene? It must be ensured that the legislative framework is the best possible in each country. Although all risks cannot be eliminated, industrialized and rich countries have the highest level of security in the world. And the situation continues to improve. Thanks to food laws, which contain all the principles of food safety, and in particular the unique principles in the world according to which the countries undertake not to export out of their territories food that does not meet the standards. And thanks to a body of inspectors, who visit different structures to authorize and control exports. Just because rich countries are the largest importers and exporters of food, they should export their security models to the world.

Thus, we believe that this model of development is the best, because it protects human health, animal health, animal welfare, ethical values of work. Producers, who have very high costs because of the standards in place, need not be at a competitive disadvantage with producers in other countries, so that the chicken producers are not at a disadvantage compared to the Chinese chicken producers. Finally, rich countries should ensure that imported food is as safe as the food it produces. In this book, we cannot go into more detail.

Do consumers have a free choice? Faced with the food and the food risk, the consumer is free in a certain way, but also constrained. It may not respect the cold chain, nor the deadline of consumption deadline, assuming its share of responsibility in the risks taken. But it may have income problems and not be able to eat the five daily recommended fruits and vegetables. The consumer, as we imagine it in colloquia, is free. Many consumers are not free simply because they are poor. They do not have the choice of their consumption, including in rich countries. Everything is complicated.

Public strategies that can have opposite effects. Example: in terms of food security, it goes without saying that "wanting cheaper than cheaper" is absurd. First, economically, this amounts to telling the buyer to abstain because tomorrow will be cheaper, and it is to engage in a consumer crisis. Then it is forcing operators to trim everything. We can reduce the number of controls, the protection of the environment and packaging, so we talk about bulk. But bulk is killing information. Public strategies can therefore have perverse effects. This pressure towards the always cheaper is deleterious and dangerous for the security.

So, where are the landmarks? All actors are looking for the theme of nutrition: operators, public authorities and consumers. Who are also the citizens? Faced with the factors of obesity (family, the television in front of which we nibble, etc.), there are clear answers: it is the procedures of education, the relations of civility (to sit at the table, to be moderate). All this is learned at school, but this training is disappearing. When, in a society, the relations of civility are degraded, then, indeed, the public decision makers are obliged to intervene in all the acts of the life in which a clash between individuals or a conflict risks to occur. Or in the ways in which an individual no longer takes into account his interest, but guided only by his desires and appetites, no longer has the superego, and the will necessary to guide and direct himself. The history of civic relations could be written as the long history of the struggle of civil societies to wrest their freedom from a power that jumps on every opportunity to legislate, regulate, and send its henchmen.

Through this debate on agribusiness, it is this big question that is at stake. For how long will the society refuse what is the very foundation of democracy, that is to say, the capacity to assume the relations of civility, which force us to exercise self-control? And willingness to handle the conflicts inherent in everyday life? Are we going to redirect ourselves to this learning that goes through school, which involves observing the law? The citizen, having no longer the strength to draw from him the keys and benchmarks that allow him to guide and orient himself, asks others to do so.

Recently, in a trendy restaurant, a waiter took an order on a minicomputer that transmitted it to the kitchen. Perhaps, soon, this computer will report the incompatibilities between the dishes likely to be too fat and the consumptions regarded as dangerous for the budgets of social security. One of these days, the restaurants will have this great idea and they will be hugely successful.

CHAPTER 6

THE FUTURE OF THE AGRIBUSINESS SECTOR

"The future will not be what will happen, but what we will do," wrote Bergson. We need to take the initiative for change in a world of many interactions. The realities, as we have seen, are not fragmented and linear; mechanical images are no longer sufficient to obtain a satisfactory representation of our world. Food is not only the fuel that allows our bodies to function and agricultural commodities are not just the crude oil from which they are extracted. What we are going to do can no longer look like mechanics; we must now reconsider the subject by placing it in the biosphere. What we are going to do is complex and living; to change, we will have to innovate and intensify research.

Yesterday again, it was about "modernizing agribusiness." Then the years that followed were marked by the turn of agro-production. The next years were those of molecular biology. Not so far, under the pressure of events marked by pollution or security problems, the field has expanded, taking into account the preservation of natural resources and the evolution of the territories, but also the questions of diet and health.

Nowadays, it is necessary to review and to imagine the possible scenarios for the future. A lot of work has been done to try to control a context that is difficult to define; various "weathers" have been considered to prepare for the right postures: faith in progress, innovations in security and comfort, in a world divided into autonomous regional blocs, global governance for sustainable development, and a fragmented world turned toward sustainable development. The models selected take into account new perceptions. The following scenarios result, highlighting the main characteristics that were retained: a specialization in generic knowledge in the life sciences, the notion of "public goods" has gained importance and the institutions must be constituted in an agribusiness "tripod," food, environment; priority is now given to food, refocused on local agribusiness, the dimension "toward sustainable development" is major.

These foresight exercises made it possible to rethink the relative place of agribusiness and other actors in a global exchange system, to take into account the role of biodiversity, to pay attention to citizens' expectations of food, and to consider health risks and climate change.

Finally, it is the structure of the agribusiness "tripod," food and environment that should be retained to establish the sectorial perspectives of the future. And six axes emerged:

- Sustainably manage and improve the environment, control the impacts of global changes and productive activities, promote a competitive "ecoagribusiness";
- Improve human nutrition, preserve the health of consumers, and understand their behavior;
- Diversify products and their uses and increase their competitiveness;
- Develop research and produce generic data for living knowledge;
- Adapt agribusiness species, practices, and production systems;
- Understand and improve the organization of actors and their strategies, analyze the challenges of public strategies, contribute to their design and evaluation, and anticipate their evolution.

Of course, there can be no question here of going into more detail. However, it must be remembered that institutional orientations need to be periodically adjusted and that it should be possible to modify and redirect public research tracks according to the future that we wish to inform and the decisions that are made by elsewhere.

It is clear, for example, that public research is a major contributor to many competitiveness clusters.

On the other hand, the intensity of the fiscal effort in the different countries is not identical according to the axes: for example, axis 1 (long-term dynamics of ecosystems) and axis 5 (innovative and sustainable farming systems, technical itineraries) each receive an average of one fifth of the budgets in rich countries; axis 4 (generic research), and axis 6 (strategy and organization of actors, public strategies) each have about one sixth of the total. It can be noted that axis 2 (that of human nutrition, with the exploration of intestinal flora) is increasing, while axis 3 (production chain–processing–distribution) is decreasing. Also, a special emphasis in rich countries is on China, India, and Brazil, on the one hand, and, on the other hand, on the Mediterranean countries.

Finally, it should be noted that researchers do not remain in their "ivory tower": the improvement of the transfer and the valuation of results is a constant concern.

Research institutions sometimes criticized should continue their perpetual transformation, using the prospective. They must be used to better understand the future: some may perceive the environment as a priority, others may highlight the food and some, even, can put far behind agribusiness in the strict sense. It would be a great mistake to "sacrifice" them, as some people recommend, probably by educational provocation. The "tripod" is a simple and robust figure that allows the greatest number of people to understand interrelationships; it can also give access to a richer representation of natural, economic, and societal phenomena to all those who have a conception that is focused exclusively on agribusiness.

From there, it must be taken into account that interrelated interrelationships are becoming more and more obvious about climate change; This is how the international markets for greenhouse gas emission allowances were born. This results in stimulation for research and innovation in the industries concerned. Should agribusiness be left out, on the pretext that the agricultural players are extremely scattered? It must be possible to involve agribusiness in the fight against greenhouse gases by imagining the means of regrouping allowing it to access the CO_2 markets.

This would stimulate, including financial, stimulation for an improved agribusiness. As this is a complex act that also affects water, soils, and biodiversity, it is a positive "reaction chain" that would be encouraged. Far from opposing intensive and organic agribusiness, as is often done without much questioning, we would have to promote new, more productive farming practices to "save hectares" and more intensive to "save energy resources." Let us dare to say that the production of ecologically intensive productive technologies is needed instead. Keeping in mind that agriculture is the photosynthesis-based activity that captures solar energy and produces biomass.

An "ecoagribusiness" must create new professions in the biomass industry, by reducing greenhouse gas emissions, by gradually replacing the use of chemical inputs with methods that make use of the photosynthesis, and using the capacity of production (and the forest) to hold CO_2. That is how the second generation of biofuels should be, within a few years, new organic liquid fuels based on wood cellulose, straw, and organic waste. Incentives already provided for nonfood agro-production, biomaterials, and biofuels should be increased, subject to undoubtedly positive ecobalance, and complemented by exemplary behavior by individual countries, among others, characterized by use of biofuels and recyclable and biologically degradable materials obtained from renewable crops. Interprofessional actions should be stimulated and encouraged in this regard.

Some countries may feel excluded from this kind of effort, given a natural situation that allows for relatively high and regular production and relatively limited future food needs. This would obviously be a misinterpretation, since we now know that we have to think of "network" and "system," even though many decisions must be made locally. On the contrary, we could discover distinctive interests in these situations: despite strong uncertainties, we know that the food needs of some rich countries will drop globally in the coming decades, while they will increase significantly in Oceania, and they will double in America. Latin America, that they will be multiplied by 2.5 in Asia and by five in Africa.

We must understand that the fight against climate change and access to water must be an opportunity to anticipate the reorientation of agribusiness models. Land pressure, agribusiness, food, and nonfood production can be modulated: trade movements offsetting deficits and food surpluses, changes in diets (including prioritizing food strategies rather than farming mechanisms: subsidize the consumption of such food products for such consumers rather than subsidize the production of such agricultural productions of such producers), movements on the price of energy, movements between monetary blocks.

Increasingly aware of these phenomena, producers know that they must listen. What they will do, locally, where they are located, is not obvious. In rich countries, the myth of "the eternal order of the fields" is scarcely gone; perhaps it is more present in the "mind" of nonproducers than in the producers themselves! These are certainly much more marked by the nurturing function of which they felt responsible during the second half of the last century, while many of the urbanists do not imagine the technical progress of which they were capable.

And now even this nurturing function no longer seems able to support the producers, at a time when consumers spend relatively less of their income to feed themselves. Worse, the "productivity" model is frightening and the vicious circle is triggered, making agribusiness guilty of climate disruption, stagnation in developing countries or "junk food." We must rebuild the raison d'être of the producers. We have just seen that they can be essential contributors to the "public good" of combating climate change. They are also capable of initiatives to anticipate the agricultural goods they must produce in order to meet the future demands of citizens' food products. They are looking for what they need to do.

This raises the recurring question of the nature of agricultural products for food in the future. It must be considered here again that in many agricultural regions of the world, producers are organizing themselves, using scenario models, to understand their future. This is the case in the field crop regions, where the biofuel plants now appear. Thus, efforts have been made in recent years at the initiative of the regional chambers to understand what will be the agricultural production by attempting an answer to the question of what will be produced from now on.

And we realize very quickly that the answers are far from simple. It was first necessary to identify "final" consumers, who today "destroy" foods whose agricultural origins are Norman, and those who will "destroy" them tomorrow. Then we should have to look for the factors that influence the evolution of the diet, and proceed to a reasoned simplification of the explanations. Two major variables have been identified: overall income growth and the distribution of income among the population. In fact, the influx of additional income does not have the same effect on food expenditure, depending on whether it is for groups with limited incomes or for the better-off groups.

Other "motor" variables were taken into account: lifestyle and food consumption (composition and way of taking meals, increase in women paid work, decrease in household size), the "nutrition-health" (obesity, voluntary government strategy, recommendation of national nutrition health plans), consumer requirements (safety and perception of food risk, quality and demand, but also breathlessness of signs of quality, taste, ethics); demographic perspectives (aging, immigration, and changing ethnic proportions) ...

The weight of certain variables has been put into perspective, such as the share of agricultural products in food expenditure, which is constantly decreasing (the price of agricultural raw materials has been divided by two, food products are more elaborate, catering out of home is developing). And some poorly understood behaviors have been given quite interesting explanations: generation effects have been highlighted.

In the food sector, a generation is marked by the behavior it adopts at twenty-five, the average age of the couple; the "deprivation" generation and the "rationing" generation opened the ball. The "refrigerators" generation benefited from better product preservation. The "household robot" generation was able to take advantage of timesaving in meal preparation, which again decreased with the "hypermarket" generation. Then the people of the generation "food services" have become accustomed to consume prepared meals, preferring to devote their free time to other activities than cooking. And the hard discount generation has become unfaithful to brands, "zappers," and no longer respect meal times.

These points are far from being anecdotal for agribusiness: after being strongly structured throughout the rich countries, will it not be more formatted by the combination consumer–distributor–processor; the combination itself very marked by the changing purchasing power of low-income groups?

Four scenarios have been devised and can be classified according to the economic growth, on the one hand, and according to the decrease or, on the contrary, the accentuation of the inequalities, on the other hand. The "trend" scenario is central: it maintains the current mode of income distribution and is governed by soft growth of more than one point five.

In the "transition from other industrial countries to the United States" scenario, overall growth is brighter, but gaps have widened between population groups; wealthier classes are turning more to commercial catering, prepared meals, seafood and fruits and vegetables; lower income groups consume more inexpensive products such as sugar, vegetable oil, and poultry. The increase in calories consumed (vegetable oil, sugar, and sugary drinks) is not combated by any nutritional strategies.

In the "crisis" scenario, growth is weak and consumption inequalities are amplified. It is the "ready to eat" that is developing, rather than catering: the production and retail industries are adapting and segmenting the food market even more. The "Nordic" scenario is where overall food expenditure is growing the most; economic growth is important and highly redistributive strategies are at work. Low-income groups "pull" the food market. Nutritional concerns are considered by public authorities, which plays a proactive role facilitated by economic growth: seafood, poultry, fruits and vegetables are acclaimed, raw, or processed, at the expense of fat and starchy foods.

This exercise highlights the different response capabilities of countries according to the current structure of agro-production. It is clear that the regions' margin of maneuver is more limited than that, characterized by diversity and robustness capable of better accepting movements, whatever their size.

In any case, we can see that the process, initiated locally by the producers, makes it possible to orient future agricultural production according to all the actors, even if the behavior of the latter is guided by considerations far removed from the act of agro-production.

What will be the companies between the raw agricultural product and the food? The strategies that the other actors will carry out constitute, for the producers, as many external variables for the orientation of the agricultural productions. It is clear that the enterprises of economic patriotism affect production all over the world: joint ventures in Bangladesh, a Muslim country to produce and market low-cost, ultranutrient yogurts, part of the financing being developed through microcredit of banks, "lender of hope."

At the same time, several companies agree to support the project of organic yogurts led by their subsidiaries in the United States, Asia, and Europe, using industrial sites promised closure. Micro credit in a developing country on one side; organic yogurts in developed countries using communication methods that avoid the mainstream media and play on the closeness between the "dairy cow" and the consumer of "organic" products on the other.

In addition, other firms are continuing to expand by opening and closing plants around the world. As we can see, their strategies materialize geographically in many parts of the world; the rulers have become "nomads." Large firms stand out from national basis. They direct their food — and therefore agricultural — activities where they find growth, whatever their source: consumption of luxury goods for some, consumption of commodities for others. The old idea of food self-sufficiency can no longer alone explain the movements of firms. There is a simultaneous increase in imports and exports, while the international activity of firms also results in their direct investments abroad. In Canada, for example, 60 percent of the food demand is satisfied by national companies; 15 percent comes from imports and 25 percent is from local subsidiaries of foreign multinational firms that have found it attractive to locate in different countries.

As we can see, a world of a hundred or so production companies worldwide regulating its activity by seeking all kinds of markets, but also taking into account variables as diverse as competition or taxation, resources infrastructures, raw materials and labor, or the business climate (administrative facilities, professional organizations, the fight against corruption). These multinational companies optimize their transportation and storage costs, exploit differences in legislation and standards, play on differences in natural conditions, and so on. If it is desirable to promote these types of companies, it is a total openness to the international that should be promoted.

At the local level, these companies are few: fewer than ten on average. Small and medium-sized enterprises are much more numerous and less open to innovation and internationalization: some of them will be driving forces in the concentration movements; others will not seek this type of development and will wish to remain in an "important artisan" size. Just like the very many very small companies, which will privilege the "short circuits." These small- and medium-sized businesses and very small businesses can only grow by innovating and exporting; many of them will choose to focus on their industrial "excellence" by specializing in private label brands.

We think it is important to recommend caution in terms of communication: is it really adroit to repeat — since very recently — that agribusiness has grown to an average of several thousand enterprises in developed countries? Is it appropriate to "inflate" the figures of the production industry with the help of craft enterprises, of which one third have no employees, if we look at the population of enterprises with fewer than twenty employees? It all depends on the objective, obviously. Would it not be better to understand that there are a thousand food groups on average in rich countries: seven hundred local groups and three hundred foreign groups? A thousand industrial groups on average that account for three quarters of the total industrial and artisanal agribusiness employment?

We would then perceive differently the questions of relations between actors; those of industrial processing groups with supermarkets and catering; those of food artisans with short and local circuits; those of the producers of "grand mix" products (cereals and milk, via collecting organisms, often cooperative) with the industrial groups; those of organic producers, etc.

The "relief" taken from the citizens by the question of agricultural cooperation would also be perceived with another acuity: in the consolidated turnover of certain cooperatives, one finds both the sales of pesticides and that of organic food products. The understanding of the connection between the food and the raw agricultural product could be clearer to nonspecialists; at the same time, knowledge of agricultural activity could be refreshed: societal and spatial planning issues would not emerge in the same way.

It should be remembered that the analysis of the average of industrialized countries includes a large artisanal and commercial sector of very small enterprises and small enterprises with fewer than twenty employees. Admittedly, they induce "territorialized" production in the vast majority of industrialized countries. But these companies mainly derive their income from the consumption of residents and tourists present; two categories whose source of income often does not come from the territory in question. Indeed, by definition, tourists have earned their income elsewhere, which is also the case for a growing part of the population: pensioners, who have built up their pension rights elsewhere than in the country where they live now. These populations generate service activities. It is therefore possible to develop employment in regions that do not necessarily shine by their industrial performance.

The ripple effect of the industry is not necessarily to look for a region that is prosperous. Just as these countries constitute competitiveness clusters, in particular to strengthen their export capacities, they could be wise to set up quality of life and services poles to drain the income of the present: tourists and pensioners who benefit from income redistribution. Thus, these countries would cover themselves with "clusters" or "poles": poles of competitiveness, poles of quality of life and services, poles of rural excellence. This is what the future of producers will be less brutally than in the form sometimes used: five hundred thousand peasants on average per country or one hundred and fifty thousand agro-managers.

Still, we must not cheat with the real conditions: certainly, the retirement age often leads in industrialized countries, the return to rural areas but these countries, where one commune out of two no longer have trade, are often weakened; the disappearance of a doctor or the cessation of activity of a craftsman, who has also reached retirement age, are often the mark of decline. In the same way, the fact that hundreds of thousands of business executives will cease their activity in the coming years is not automatically the sign of a rebirth through their transmission: it is estimated that half of them have no value.

Three scenarios emerge from there: the scenario of continuity; the scenario of the age war; and the scenario of the golden age of gray hair. The first would be marked by the continuity of the "sprawl" of space, by the fact that only the "beautiful cases" are taken over, by a handcraft in difficulty, by a collapse of the production, and by a significant presence of seniors looking for the sea and the sun. The second scenario is worse. It's the age of everyone for themselves: "small paradises" for retirees with the means, small bosses obliged to continue working because the valuation of their company would give them too small savings to ensure their retirement, a production model in crisis to the point that there is more maintenance of nature and landscapes.

The last scenario benefits from more positive inflections: birth and immigration revival, deterrence of the double residence with constitution of a better single accommodation and fewer trips, economy driven by the "face-to-face" with a flourishing craft, access of small and medium-sized companies to public markets... In short, a living and flexible fabric of very small businesses and small- and medium-sized enterprises, with a multiplicity of retirees.

As we see in this exercise, there is no choice for agribusiness: only the last scenario does not predict its collapse. It is therefore the one toward which it would have to orient itself. At the end of this chapter, let us rather try to propose a probable image of what we could observe in the years to come.

This caricature, mixture of tendencies and wishes, is there to arouse the expression of what everyone will have to do. Obviously, what everyone will do will be different. Not only because many factors are ignored, but also because the will of some may not be compatible with those of others. The reflections engendered, backed up by the timetable of which we will recall a few steps, could inspire the programs of action of each other.

Is it legitimate, and especially useful, to intervene in agriculture in a world in constant motion? As absurd as it may seem at first glance to some, accustomed to the existence of specific strategies in production, this question is nevertheless subject to debate. For some liberal theorists, whose arguments are taken up by the new major agricultural countries with significant comparative advantages (primarily in the Cairns group and Brazil), full liberalization of the productive sector would be virtuous.

In the absence of disruptive mechanisms, the market would find its own equilibrium through the "price" variable, whose downward adjustment, because of increased competition, would benefit the final consumer, and in particular to the inhabitants of the poorest countries. At the same time, the opening of regional markets would stimulate production in these less developed countries, increase capital inflows, and promote the emergence of new activities.

This antiphon, which is now commonly heard in international negotiation forums, is not relevant. Certainly, a world "folded in on itself" in agricultural matters would not be advantageous for a country as rich as it is, nor for a coherent regional set like Alena. And this both for defensive reasons (the lack of guaranteed food self-sufficiency, making it essential to use imports) and offensive (trade of agricultural products, raw as processed, is a source of enrichment). If full protectionism is therefore unthinkable, radical liberalization seems, on the contrary, totally untimely, for both economic and extraeconomic reasons.

From an economic point of view, the specific characteristics of agricultural supply and demand favor chronic market instability, which can undermine the principle of food security and greatly erode farm incomes. Several elements are advanced to support this thesis of the natural instability of agricultural markets:

1. The inelasticity of global demand for agricultural products, responding weakly to price changes;
2. The rigidity of the supply of agricultural products, depending on natural cycles of production that it is impossible or difficult to hasten in order to respond to a sudden change in demand;
3. The high elasticity, on the other hand, of the supply of each agricultural product in the medium term, producers being able to change their crops quite easily at each new production cycle;
4. Uncertainty about the supply of products available at a given time, both quantitatively and qualitatively, due to the unpredictability of natural and economic hazards

The so-called Cobweb model accounts for this natural instability in agricultural markets resulting in sharp price level fluctuations. Faced with two uncertainties — on the selling price of agricultural products and the quantity likely to be sold at the end of the cycle — producers tend to choose a lower level of production than they would have chosen in a certain situation. The demonstration can thus be made that perfectly free markets do not lead, in agricultural matters, to an optimal allocation of factors.

From an extraeconomic point of view, full liberalization of the markets does not seem desirable either. The multifunctional nature of agribusiness means that the primary activity, besides a function of producing goods valued by the market, also provides services that are of interest to society as a whole, or at least a fraction of the wider population. That the only agricultural population (maintenance of rural territories, maintenance of open and diversified agricultural landscapes, preservation of biodiversity, attenuation of air pollution due to the consumption of CO_2 by plants...).

However, these services are not valued at fair value by the market because of their nature as public goods. They therefore require support from public authorities to respond to a social demand. From this perspective, agricultural products are not like other goods.

These economic and noneconomic reasons therefore call for the maintenance of regulation of agricultural markets by appropriate public strategies. Strategies carried out at the level of the different regions of the world are part of this perspective and could, subject to a slight reorientation, respond perfectly to the objectives of market stabilization and compensation for positive externalities induced by agricultural activity, if these goals were clearly displayed and shared.

The first pillar of these strategies favors a goal of income support to the detriment of the fight against market instability. Recent developments, however, tend to point to greater policy intervention in risk management.

Thus, an ambitious crop insurance program, supposed to eventually cover all productions, is being implemented in many countries. These trends point to a reinforcement of security mechanisms. These devices, which have the notable advantage of being compatible with the legislation in force in commercial institutions, are now largely favored by the United States, which plans to transit through its medium the bulk of its revenues. Public support for production.

The second pillar of these mechanisms, which has been gradually ramping up, could perfectly meet the objective of remuneration of positive externalities desired by the company. To this end, it should focus on the granting of permanent direct aid for efforts made by producers to provide environmental or territorial public services that go beyond the standards in force. As such, these supports should be delivered under contracts, probably multiannual, between producers and the public authorities with clear identification of the indicators on which they can be based for the achievement of one or another objective.

A reorientation of these strategies in this twofold perspective would thus make it possible to fully satisfy the two objectives of market stabilization and remuneration of public amenities that it seems legitimate, and effective, to pursue in agricultural matters. Neither protectionist nor ultraliberal, the position that the producing countries must defend in international fora is therefore to advocate on a regional scale for a balanced market framework model to achieve these objectives. Far from envisaging a dismantling of mechanisms, it is toward a strategy of this type that it is essential today to turn.

The mark of current mechanisms will still be strong on agribusiness for a while, and then it will decline. Is not it desirable? Is it not advisable to reduce production aid in countries where it becomes economically viable on its own (and remains liveable and equitable)? Should not developing countries be able to draw inspiration from the past success of the strategic mechanisms peculiar to the industrialized countries, particularly to regulate rural exodus and emigration to developed countries by major world regions?

In some rich countries, the mechanisms that work today are such that, if the subsidies to producers were removed, their income would be zero. This means that the aid thus granted is reflected in the prices of raw agricultural products: these falls, which benefit the food industries, which benefit from a secure local supply. The first industrial sector in these countries continues, while continuing to invest and generating a trade surplus. And at the level of European countries, whose territory is half the size of that of the United States, the agribusiness system manages to feed one hundred fifty million citizens more than other Atlantic. These countries each export more processed food than the United States.

Should we really "sacrifice production" and divert subsidies to other uses? On the other hand, it is obvious that public expenditure on production will fall: the direct influence of the food industry on the primary sector will become more pressing while simultaneously, the food industry will rather meet the pressures of large retailers. The gradual distortion of the agribusiness system will weigh on the territories (nature), while interactions with consumers will significantly change their health.

At the same time, everyone's lives will be modified by the intensification of nonfood production (unless the ecobalance is not as good, and we come to declare that the development of biofuels was not only one way of giving another form to Western agricultural surpluses...). So, let's dare a few traits, for the G7 countries.

A third of these countries will be covered by forests (CO_2 traps). The equivalent of half of the forest will consist of other natural areas and artificial spaces. The rest will be occupied by the production. Two thirds of the producers will be professionals: they will exploit 90 percent of the agricultural surface.

For a long time now, 80 percent of the young people who settle hold at least a bachelor's degree; but they are only an average of a few thousand per year to settle. The size of companies to take over is becoming increasingly important in developed countries: cooperatives may have to become "producers" themselves in their youth assistance programs. With few exceptions, they will be better producers than food processors; they will also make agribusiness for nonagricultural purposes.

This trend implies stimulating the restructuring and restructuring of cooperatives, probably differentiating according to the size of the structures: the many small wine cooperatives, for example the large production cooperatives, cannot be treated in the same way.

The natural and logistical disparities will become more apparent. The large diagonals in the developed countries will be even more marked by cereal monocultures (and therefore less and less grassland and animals, which will lead to an impoverishment of organic matter and the endangerment of soil fertility). In particular, we will have the following distribution: dairy cow zone, suckler cow zone, horse zone, sheep zone, goat zone, pigs and chicken zone, fat poultry zone. Half of the orchard will be concentrated, one quarter in some areas and one tenth in others. The disadvantaged areas will not change and will remain the same. Irrigation will certainly be done differently, but always in the same areas today. Producers will be "full time" in some countries.

A "trilogy" is desirable: rural areas dominated by net agriculture, with extension of "working" channels around a highly professionalized world. In contrast, other regions in the world, deeply weakened in demography. And the most complex: interstitial agribusiness, in metropolitan areas.

In one part of the diagonal, we find most of the major agro-production companies; in others, small (with a significant weight of viticulture). On average, three hundred groups of more than five hundred employees or foreign capital, representing thousands of companies per country on average, will gather hundreds of thousands of employees by country. Among them, ten groups will concentrate 20 percent of total employment and twenty groups 30 percent on average.

Three quarters of companies will still have fewer than twenty employees. These eight thousand craft enterprises per country will represent only 10 percent of the workforce in the sector and 5 percent of turnover. An average of two thousand five hundred of them will have four or fewer employees. They will be comparable to a good number of agricultural businesses that have definitely left the family farm model. Of the eight thousand artisanal enterprises on average per country, two thousand five hundred will be in the meat and sausage sector, two thousand in the wine sector (many of which with export activity), and one thousand in the dairy and cheese sector.

National markets in rich countries are now "mature": global growth will not increase unless export success. Hence the interest, but also the limits, of the various export sector plans, trade shows, the "export kit" or the Export Strategy Support Committee around the world. But the growth of this or that company can be brightened if it innovates. Innovation is stimulated by many structures, so that restructuring may be important, benefiting from the accelerating effects of development capital specialists in both private and cooperative structures. Feeding methods, management of agricultural and food risks, and qualitative or normative evolutions will be opportunities for differentiation and growth.

Production and agribusiness will thus be transformed, by renewing themselves in rich countries more than elsewhere by destruction and creation (the examples of companies — which in a few years have become world specialists in analysis — are very stimulating from this point of view.), under the pressure of the distribution systems, whether those of the large distribution or the short circuits.

The price will become more secondary in the purchase decision (as we know, the relative expenditure of the consumers drops: they dedicate today fewer than 15 percent of their income to the products of the food and less than 3 percent to the agricultural products). The attention to the person will become major again: nowadays arguments will increase in the domains "health," "nature," and "social and ethical behavior," with a growing awareness connecting the individual to the entire biosphere.

We have begun rediscovering networks that surround agribusiness by asking the question: What do you think of when you push your shopping cart? As if by echo, the person pushing the cart will always pass before the cart that it pushes in the future. Let all the actors say it!

CHAPTER 7

THE SECTOR HAS BEEN ABLE TO CHANGE

To note that the agribusiness of the G7a countries has, in recent years, become the world leader, does not allow, of course, to affirm that it will be able to respond to contemporary global issues. Nevertheless, this observation is an essential preliminary for three reasons: firstly, by demonstrating its ability to adapt and to diversify, agribusiness in rich countries appears today as an unstable player in the global economy. Today, more than ever, the environment is in perpetual motion.

Secondly, these production industries have, overall, been able to meet the expectations of consumers: alongside mass production, which continues to play a key role, the agribusiness sector has taken into account, more and more, in recent years, certain consumer health, quality and safety requirements, which, although evolving in the future, will become stronger.

Finally, this economic sector has taken the measure of the world in which it operates: the structural surplus of the balance of foreign trade of these countries in the field of agribusiness for some time is proof of this. In the face of successive reforms in agricultural strategies in developed countries, the agribusiness industries have so far managed to cope with the internationalisation of trade and investment. Agribusiness has, from the beginning, demonstrated a strong ability to adapt. The industry is defined as the industrial activity that transforms raw materials coming mainly from agriculture and fishing into products intended for food and feed. It is therefore integrated into the agro-production system, which goes from the production of the means of production for agriculture to distribution and even consumption.

A first transformation of the agricultural products intervenes from the beginning of the last century, which develops after the Second World War in the animal, then vegetable sector. But it is only in the middle of the thirty glorious years that the process of industrialisation of the agro-production sector begins, with a joint acceleration of capital-labour substitution and labour productivity. Development in this sector has been based both on a qualitative transformation of production methods and a change in the nature of manufactured products.

While the industrial fabric in the industrialised world was facing a severe crisis during the 1970s, the agro-production industries continued to grow, particularly in the bakery and meat sectors. Subsequently, a notable weakening of productivity gains has particularly affected agribusiness, whose growth in value added in value has slowed sharply. Despite shortcomings in the introduction of new competitiveness factors, these industries have established themselves as the leading industrial sector, bringing even some countries to the forefront of the world's exporting agribusiness powers.

Sectorial competitiveness rested, among other things, on the diversification of the distribution of the industry across all the territories concerned. This diversification of the sector has two aspects. The first concerns the variety and heterogeneity of the industrial branches represented within this sector. In addition to the traditional distinction between primary and secondary processing industries, nine food industry families are usually distinguished by the official nomenclature of official activity in rich countries. These families meat, fish, fruit and vegetables, fat, starch grain, animal feed, beverage, dairy, and finally 'miscellaneous' industries encompass an infinite variety of sub-sectors and products.

It is therefore necessary, when talking about agribusiness, to talk about production industries in the plural.

This diversity is reflected in the institutional presentations on foreign trade of agribusiness products. Thus, in addition to the distinction between agricultural products and food products, about twenty products are presented among which: fish, tobacco, soy, plants, livestock, canned goods, fresh fruits, temperate fruits, products milling, oilseeds, sugar, poultry meat, cattle, dairy products, cereals, wines and spirits…

The second aspect concerns the structure of agro-production companies.

The 'industrial sector' of the cooperative sector is traditionally distinguished in different countries. On average, the industrial sector groups several thousand enterprises with more than ten employees, fourteen per cent of them having fewer than five hundred employees and forty-seven per cent under fifty. The vast majority of these small and medium enterprises have a family capital. If they already belong to groups, they continue to function as independent companies. The agro-production sectors of about seven industrialised countries also comprise a large network of small and medium-sized enterprises.

In addition to these 'industrial enterprises', the cooperative sector is strongly present in this activity. The precise estimation of the weight of the co-operation in the agro-production sector is quite variable according to the parameters used: first and second transformation, whether or not the subsidiaries of the cooperatives are taken into account in the official statistics, integration or not of certain sectors such as tobacco… The co-operation sector therefore represents, depending on the branches and criteria selected, between seventeen per cent and thirty-three per cent of the turnover of agro-production. While welcoming the specificities of agricultural co-operation and the link that exists with agricultural upstream, it should be noted that agricultural cooperatives have today become, for the most part, real enterprises in the G20 countries because of the market. Of the first agro-production groups, about one third of cooperative groups.

The Three Businesses of Agricultural Co-operation in Rich Countries (Subsidiaries Included)

	Average turnover by country (billions of dollars)	Average market share (%)	Total average market (turnover in billions of dollars)
UPSTREAM: collect and wholesale activity	170	57	300
DOWNSTREAM: Industrial transformation of agribusiness production	200	25	792
Agricultural and rural supply services	50	60	90
TOTAL	420	142	1182

There are usually a few major world groups (five French, one French-Italian versus thirty-two American, thirteen English, nineteen Japanese and seven Dutch), the size or national-sized enterprises and small and medium-sized family businesses

Key Figures of Agribusiness Industries

Industrial sectors	Average number of companies (thousand)	Average waged staff (billions)	Average turnover (billions)	Average added value (billions)	Average investment excluding contributions
Meats	1,463	117.8	178.3	25.9	3.5
Fish	173	11.9	14.9	2.6	0.5
Fruits and vegetables	194	22.2	32.4	6.2	1.3
Fat elements	30	4.2	13.2	2	0.3
Dairy products	415	59.4	136.9	18.9	3.3
Grain	193	12.4	28.5	6.1	1.8
Animal food	306	17.8	56.6	6.6	1
Diverse food products	991	92.1	154.2	38	5.2
Beverages	492	40.2	95.3	24.8	4
Total	4,257	378	710.3	131.1	20.9

A more detailed examination of the structure of the agro-production sector reveals its role in regional planning in industrialised countries. On average, ten thousand agribusiness firms have fewer than twenty employees: these represent ten per cent of agribusiness employment and five per cent (or thirty-nine billion dollars on average) of the turnover of all industries in agro-production. They are about twenty per cent on average in the beverage industries and ten per cent on average in the milk industry, due to the establishment of small businesses in winemaking and cheese making. These economic entities are scattered throughout the G20 countries and are much more numerous in some regions and others, traditional areas of concentration of the food industry.

This industry is spread over all the countries concerned and represents on average twenty-eight per cent of its jobs. Very present in urban areas, it contributes to the industrialisation of rural areas.

As such, industries in agro-production have become today 'the obligatory intermediary between the field and the plate.' They feed on raw materials at the farmer who proves to be their main supplier: this relationship with agricultural upstream has evolved considerably for a long time. At first, the emergence of the agro-production sector somewhat 'confiscated' certain activities that were carried out within farms. Subsequently, there was a strong industrialisation of production, encouraged by the agricultural industries. This movement has led to pressure from the agricultural upstream production sector, whose integration contracts for a given period are an example. Does this mean that the marketability of trade between these two sectors has been questioned?

It is difficult to think for several reasons: first of all, producers still own their means of production generally, selling goods and not their labour power. In addition, the organisation of supply (through producer organisations, for example) helps to balance this balance of power. Finally, there is a significant change in attitudes: the downstream of agro-production is better taken into consideration. While until recently, the industry was responsible for transforming the agricultural raw material, now agribusiness is responsible for providing the raw material that meets the requirements of consumption.

Today, seven out of ten food products are purchased in supermarkets and hypermarkets, which have become the first customers in the agro-production sector. The conflicting relations between the production and distribution industries, especially the supermarket chains, are easily explained: if the former seek to make the most of the profitability of the processing of their products, the second wants to reduce this added value to increase its own margin.

The development of large and medium-sized stores has had two important consequences for the sector: in the first place, the number of customers of this sector has been considerably reduced by the concentration of large-scale retail channels. This development has resulted in increased pressure on prices and accelerated the restructuring of the agro-industrial fabric by the disappearance of the least competitive companies. Secondly, the growth of large and medium-sized retailers have also led to product or service requirements: these include the reputation of the products, their quality, the ability of the distributor to industrialists to decline and diversify its production and finally logistics (large and medium-sized businesses have imposed their pace on companies).

The example of the evolution of delivery deadlines for large and medium-sized agricultural products: the distribution traditionally required the delivery of products for the second day after several years ago. In recent years, this period has been reduced by twenty-four hours, with large and medium-sized businesses placing orders for the next day. In recent years, mass distribution requires delivery the same day, often before seventeen or eight o'clock. This downstream margin transfer operated by large and medium-sized retailers explain the market performance of the distribution, whose index often crossed the place of Paris by seven thousand points, the food value index capping at two thousand points.

Faced with this pressure on agro-production and the ever-increasing scale of concentration in the mass-market sector (with several mergers, the number of large and medium-sized groups in the industrialised countries is now five at ten on average), some evoke an almost identical process of concentration in the production industries. On the one hand, the combined turnover of its merged firms is, according to the countries, four times higher than that of the largest business agribusinesses. We cannot assimilate these two processes of concentration. On the other hand, it is difficult to compare the establishment of a large distribution network limited to half a dozen groups on average and the industrial structure of a sector of activity which, depending on the country, has more than four a thousand independent companies, some of which depend on their turnover of their buyer to more than ninety per cent.

Despite this context, small and medium-sized agribusiness enterprises are by no means doomed to disappear: in fact, alongside this ever more current pressure on agribusiness, the segmentation of consumer demand has increased. The cross-fertilisation of the multiple requirements of the end customer has created a multitude of 'niches', which are all development opportunities for local or innovative small and medium-sized companies. Also, relations with large retailers, even if they often remain conflictual, are sometimes conceived within the framework of a 'tailor-made' partnership considering the specificities of each one.

In addition, the manufacture of private label products may, under certain conditions (notably the respect of the commercial partner), also constitute a solution for small and medium-sized enterprises which have a good control of the production costs, but which does not do not have the capabilities to bear the increasing cost of advertising and commercial expenses in order to drive a branding strategy. Thus, without denying the dominance of large and medium-sized surfaces by various means (such as that of commercial co-operation that equates to a real blackmail to SEO, catalogue promotions...), the agro-production industries have sought to refocus their industrial strategy to circumvent this pressure, sometimes (it is true), to no avail.

In this configuration, how has the industry globally responded to consumer expectations? Food is based on three essential pillars: the nutritional base, cultural habits and economic components (income, etc.) in rich countries. The food function aims to satisfy the need to feed, with a concern for maximum hygiene, at a lower cost, but also tends to respond to the quest for pleasure that the consumer experiences in the food product.

Today, food consumption in these regions accounts for between fifteen and eighteen per cent of household budgets. The agro-production sector has managed not only to satisfy the mass consumption of food products, but also to meet (at least in large part) the expectations of consumers in terms of safety, health and quality. The agribusiness is thus significantly increased productivity and competitiveness gains.

The considerable development of processed food products at the expense of undeveloped products is due not only to changes in the way of life (saving time in the preparation of meals, the distance of consumers from places of production of foodstuffs) but also to the sharp drop in prices of standardised products and the overall rise in revenues. This 'period of adaptation of the diet to the standards of the code of life given by the urbanisation, the economy of time and the society of consumption' ended a few years ago. Although the sector has therefore followed the development pattern of the 'Thirty-first', it has since flourished in a new food landscape whose symbol was mass consumption and later segmentation of markets.

In this respect, food safety and quality have become non-negotiable requirements for the sector. While mass production has given way to market segmentation, food consumption has been marked, among other things, by the emergence of new expectations in terms of taste, freshness, safety, health, and cultural content. Linked to the terroir and to specific know-how. The shortcomings of the various food safety regulations will have to be highlighted.

Food has now become a hot topic, the consumer requires, in this regard, an irreproachable security. A preliminary, consumer safety, as well as the diversity of products, do not have sacrificed in the development of the agro-production sector. Food products are healthier, safer today than yesterday. And if crises are triggered, it is because today the controls are more effective.

It should be remembered that listeriosis cases were divided by three, that is three points' eight cases on average per million inhabitants in the industrialised countries. In addition, collective food poisoning has averaged between three hundred and thirty-four and four hundred and seventy-eight outbreaks per year in the West, with about eight thousand patients per country. Even if these figures are underestimated, they nevertheless reflect a worsening of the situation, especially taking into account the increase in the tonnages of foodstuffs manufactured in circulation and the increasing number of meals taken in the past.

This security concern does not date from recent crises. It has always been an essential determinant in the manufacture of the food product: however, for years it has become the priority for agribusiness industries. So today there is only one major concern that becomes totally obsessive: that of food security. Some believe that this 'zero defect' concern in food is not normal, noting that tobacco or even cars are hundreds of times more dangerous than food: such logic cannot be guaranteed.

Indeed, if everyone is (or should be) aware of the risks involved in smoking or taking his vehicle, no one expects to put his life in danger by the consumption of a food product, supposed to satisfy a need essential nutrition. However, we must also avoid the inverse reasoning, totally excessive, of exonerate the consumer from any responsibility: thus, we know that the raw milk cheese can, in certain specific cases, present risks for specific populations (pregnant women, the elderly...). It is therefore imperative to prevent these populations by informing them as well as possible (information campaign, dissemination in schools and universities, information by the medical and paramedical professions...). It does not seem appropriate, however, to condemn this product for tens of thousands of consumers.

Thus, during the last crisis of 'chicken dioxin', honesty requires acknowledging, on the one hand, that an accident, and more likely fraud is at the origin and that, on the other hand, no case of human contamination could be detected. In addition, several countries have adapted their food safety legislation for human food products to put an end to the malfunctions that can occur in food.

The new mechanisms for monitoring the sanitary quality of products are based, first and foremost, on the standards for strengthening health surveillance of products intended for humans. These texts create independent structures, which are now the national tools for assessing the health and nutritional risks of food. The health surveillance systems set up by these standards also include structures that replace the former public health networks and provide for the coordination of several health and safety agencies in health products. Secondly, the various agricultural orientation regulations aim, in particular, to strengthen the controls of services in the countries along the value chains, and in particular their upstream ones, and tend to increase, in particular, the coherence of the different systems of official identification of the quality of foodstuffs (biovigilance device...) according to the country.

It is important to remember that food risk management, the public service mission par excellence, is a prerogative strategy that comes under the executive powers, under the control of legislative powers. This mission is to match the recommendations made by the experts in charge of the scientific risk assessment, the means of all kinds that the community, the companies and the producers can devote to the control of the risks, the objectives in terms of levels defined by the decision makers and too broad public information. In this new context, it is up to specific food structures, in co-operation with the other administrations concerned by food safety, to carry out these public service tasks.

Alongside the official controls, the important work of the profession in food safety should be commended. The implementation of an effective traceability strategy, the development of guides to good hygienic practices validated by the various branches, the taking into account of the method of hazard analysis critical control points (general method which is to dissect a food process to define it the key points of a risk analysis and remedying them) as well as the explosion in the number of certified sites attest to the real will of the sector in industrialised countries to achieve irreproachable food safety, professionals being aware that it is impossible today to compromise on such imperatives.

In addition to this safety requirement, the consumer is more and more attentive to the quality of the products. This quality objective does not date from the last years since, even during the 'Fordism' period of the agribusiness industries, certain markets were specifically devoted to 'quality' products. Nevertheless, if the niche of high-end products has expanded, the consumer expects today, even on basic products, a minimum of quality. For example, next to the label chicken whose production is growing, it is now unthinkable to offer an industrial chicken that does not respect certain organoleptic qualities. The agribusiness enterprises thus modify their organisation to improve the quality of their products, while trying to reduce their costs, the consumer having become accustomed to believing that the food product should be systematically cheap.

Agro-production industries are adopting more and more standards certified by external organisations to achieve these objectives. For example, one out of two dairy companies has a reference certification and thirty per cent hold standards guaranteeing their seriousness. In addition, sixty-one per cent of agro-production companies are developing 'quality' approaches.

In addition, the strengthening of quality control is manifest in the organisation of work; thus one in two agro-production companies has a full-time executive for this task, and one in four has created a quality control post.

In addition to these company certification procedures, which attest to the establishment of a quality assurance system in accordance with international standards, agribusiness production industries have engaged in product certification as a label or certification of conformity: this orientation has become essential today in the industrial strategies of most structures. In addition, the establishment of the labels is a good example of a sector strategy, which is to say of commitments negotiated from the agricultural producer to the distributor, aiming at the guarantee of a superior, clearly identifiable quality by the consumer. On average, there are nearly five hundred labels. This system of signs of quality reinforces the traceability mechanisms that have proved decisive during the events. Quality is at the heart of business development strategies. This new imperative is one of the keys to success in local and international markets.

Agro-production has also taken into account the international dimensions of the food markets. No one is astonished today about successive records of surpluses in the trade balance. However, the phenomenon only appeared in its time and did not impose itself durably until a few years ago. Indeed, there was a time when the industrialised world was heavily deficient in agribusiness, and some countries sourced mainly from former colonies. The creation of regional markets has led to a reorientation of exchanges with their partners.

The global dimension of the production markets by the agribusiness industries is a fundamental fact from which two aspects can be immediately noted.

In the first place, the importance of regional markets for foreign trade in the production sector is well established. The surplus obtained between Western partners averaged $45 billion, or seventy-seven per cent of the overall surplus. Even if this volume is down by a few billion dollars (minus nine points three) the phenomenon has a structural character.

The same is true for Western exports, and imports from different regional areas (accounting for more than seventy per cent of the total). In recent years, regional exports have been fairly stable at over two thirds of rich-country exports, while intra-zone imports have played a growing role (from less than one third to more than one third).

Nevertheless, it is necessary to differentiate between agricultural products and products of production (although this distinction is sometimes based on questionable criteria). In fact, while the balance of agricultural products has steadily improved, the situation is somewhat different for agribusiness products: the intra-zone external balance, after a favourable trend, has continuously deteriorated to become negative. However, this trend has been reversed recently, with the balance of intra-regional agribusiness products becoming surplus. The share of agribusiness products in exports has increased from fifty-eight to five per cent to almost seventy per cent, reflecting the productivity, competitiveness and expansion efforts of this industry.

Secondly, the establishment of large regional food groups is indicative of the importance of regional markets for agribusiness industries. About thirty industrial groups on average are among the top hundred intra-zones, which makes these industries important intra-zone players for the number of groups. Among these regional (or even global) agro-production industries are a large number of industries of the same nationality...

Even if these groups remain insufficient both in number and in volume of turnover, agribusiness has not escaped, since the beginning of the decade, the movement of concentration that the sector has experienced in the whole world and which had begun in the Anglo-Saxon countries. The evolution of the consolidated turnover of the top 20 global groups highlights this phenomenon of concentration.

In the last fifteen years or so, there have been numerous restructurings in this sector of activity: thus, each year, nearly two hundred mergers, acquisitions and acquisitions of shares are recorded. These movements represented more than thirty billion dollars on average. The development of industrialised agro-production has benefited from the different regional constructions and agricultural strategies in particular.

Indeed, the vigorous increase in volumes produced, the fall in real producer prices, tariff unification when it exists, then the establishment of sector-specific mechanisms and the gradual dismantling of tariff barriers to trade within different single markets have all contributed to strengthening agribusiness.

From there, the international development of agro-production is, first and foremost, due to the significant increase in the exchange of agribusiness products. The acceleration of the phenomenon of globalisation has been clearly perceptible for agribusiness products, the index of exports having risen from one hundred to one hundred and thirty-seven on average per country, as against one hundred to one hundred and fifteen for world production. Internationalisation is concretised, correlatively, by the multiplication of intra-country commercial and agro-industrial establishments.

In addition, over the past fifteen years, the amount of investment in agribusiness has increased considerably worldwide. Foreign takeovers in the agribusiness industry, and even the irresistible colonisation of production, must be emphasised: faced with the financial strength of multinationals, many medium-sized family businesses have indeed been bought back...

The growth of foreign acquisitions in rich countries does not appear to have been merely cyclical, but rather to be based on substantive reasons. In the absence of real investors, size becoming a necessity in some markets, agribusiness productivity, know-how, modern equipment in the food industry, its regional export opportunities, its engineering vis-à-vis developing countries and finally the gradual removal of barriers to trade have explained and probably explain that the financial resources of the main foreign groups have spread to certain countries.

These operations, which each year amount to over a billion dollars, are sometimes the cause of some difficult situations due to the restructuring they involve. They have, however, allowed a large number of agribusiness industries, by offering them the ability to reach a critical size to be present in regional and international markets, to develop.

Settlements outside the metropolitan territory of industrialists were quite unusual. These existed in Latin America and in the former countries of the USSR. Surveys have shown about a threefold increase in the presence of some G7 countries abroad. The total investment of these countries in regional markets for agribusiness has exceeded on average two billion dollars.

Large Western firms traditionally remain the main investors abroad, which corresponds to the strategy of redeployment on the main businesses of these groups: fresh dairy products, mineral water and biscuits, all in priority to emerging countries. Southeast Asia and Latin America. This strategy is followed, to a lesser extent, by other less-rated groups for cheeses and in spirits, for example. With ten per cent of world trade, some Western countries are now the world's leading exporters of processed agribusiness products: Western agribusiness has therefore taken full advantage of its strengths (abundance, variety, quality, etc.) to cope with new, globally transformed food markets, while evolving in a context of increased trade liberalisation.

CHAPTER 8

THE PRODUCTION AND THE CONTEMPORARY CHALLENGES

The adaptability that agribusiness has shown in the face of history will be more necessary tomorrow that it will face critical issues. These are numerous and varied, but form, in fact, a very homogeneous triptych in which each element is dependent on the other two; thus, the increasing internationalization of the food exchanges, the enlargement of the regional markets, and the future international agreements, will make for example, changes in world food demand that are key to the evolution of the agribusiness sector.

But this increased internationalization of trade also concerns new technologies, which have a major impact on the future of the agribusiness sector: there is for example, the case of biotechnology and the technology of biotechnology. Information of communication whose consequences are heavy. The last, and not least, to which agro-production will have to respond is that of food safety, food quality, and the environment: these requirements have appeared, certainly, for several years, but they will reach, in the years to come, an entirely different dimension. In fact, since these requirements will not be sufficiently considered, the internationalization of markets and the immediate dissemination of information will generate immediate economic and financial sanctions, but also (let us not forget), social for the company.

Thus, the agribusiness sector will have to face the perspectives of evolution of the food markets and the agribusiness industries will then face in the coming years two fundamental trends: one concerns the increasing liberalization of trade in the food sector, the other relates to the increase of the global food demand.

These two issues are not new for this sector of activity: the agribusiness industries already had to cope with periods of growth in the world's food demand that is sometimes greater than that predicted in the past. In addition, the process of trade liberalization has already started a long time ago, and at least some institutional arrangements have been made.

Nevertheless, these issues will be imposed on the agro-production sector with a particular acuity in the years to come. For instance, several international organizations regularly carry out prospective studies on global agribusiness and the outlook for the production sector. We can say that the conclusions are to be taken with great care, given the uncertainties as to the forecasts to ten or fifteen years. Nevertheless, some conclusions help to foster the reflection on the medium-term future of the global agribusiness industry.

In developing countries, the agribusiness sector would face several changes. First of all, the global population should continue to grow as the population will reach several billion inhabitants: the increase in the world population will rise each year by more than eighty million inhabitants. In a context of global improvement, economic growth, rising incomes, and increasing urbanization, particularly in Asia and Latin America, global agricultural growth is expected to grow at a slow pace (over 1.8 per year). That is, close to zero in terms of production. A certain slowdown in world agricultural production is not negative as it reflects a lower world population growth and an increase in the number of people who have more or less reached a minimum level of food consumption. But this slowdown could be linked to the fact that populations likely to consume, more do not have enough income to increase their food demand.

In addition, international analyses show that food supplies per capita for direct human consumption, particularly in developing countries, are expected to continue to grow overall, from 2550 to

2800 calories; Africa stays away from this evolution. Food demand in developing countries is expected to grow by more than 2.6 percent per year (except for the least developed countries), which is important.

If trade in agricultural products continues to account for 10 percent of world trade, trade in processed products and livestock products could grow much faster. For example, China's demand for meat would increase by 85 percent and that of cereals by 30 percent in the next twenty years. In addition, developing countries (now globally net exporters of agricultural products) would become net importers of agricultural products and certain processed products. In addition, these countries will increasingly shift from vegetable protein-based diets to animal protein-based diets.

This fundamental change would have an extremely important consequence for industrialized agribusiness: indeed, this new volume of imports would enable rich countries, whose domestic or regional markets are stagnant, to gain access to attractive export markets and opportunities. Attractive direct investments. However, these new markets would be captured only by the United States and the Cairns Group countries because of their more attractive prices and their strategies favoring market mechanisms, especially when it comes to exports. Thus, some developed countries would be subject to strong competitive pressures that would lead to the loss of a large number of markets in the food sector. Added to this is the possible increase in the import penetration rate for regional markets, because of possible reductions in custom protection.

It is therefore important to underline the challenge for the agribusiness industry of developing food demand in the near future, particularly from developing countries. Some observers believe, of course, that today this potential danger remains relatively low given the importance of regional markets for the industrialized agribusiness sector. But such reasoning could in the short term be particularly risky for two reasons. In the first place, industrialized agribusiness trade has been losing important intrazone market shares for several months. Secondly, the increasing globalization of trade could lead to an increased emphasis on food trade with third countries, which is a real challenge for some countries that do not seem best placed, especially in terms of price, to satisfy those markets.

In other regions, the evolution of the sector is analyzed not only quantitatively but also qualitatively. As a result of the aging of the population, the increase in the female participation rate and the reduction in the size of families, consumers eating habits should continue to evolve. Time-saving food options, such as ready-to-use processed products, ready-to-eat hot dishes, delivery services and catering, will undoubtedly be more obvious in the future.

Also, the increase in trade and investment has, of course, also affected the agribusiness sector for years. At the G20 level, economic reforms by lowering institutional prices for cereals, for beef, and in the milk and dairy sector are lifesaving. Agribusiness is therefore pursuing a gradual liberalization movement, marked by an increased transfer of market support towards direct aid to producers, without these being truly decoupled... The agribusiness professionals have encouraged this development, and appear to be generally satisfied with the results obtained during those last negotiations.

Indeed, given the decline in export refunds in several countries, the approximation of agricultural prices with world prices (so unrepresentative in agriculture) allows for a reduction in raw material supply costs. The agribusiness thus improves its margins on sales made on the internal market and lowers its selling prices on the markets of third countries, thus increasing its competitiveness, while benefiting from less dependence on regional decisions regarding export refunds. The implementation of these new strategic reforms should therefore not globally create difficulty for this sector of transformation, especially since it is carried out in a context of monetary stability in a global manner.

Nevertheless, the agribusiness sector will have to expect a sharp reduction in supplies, especially the oilseed industry, because of the drop in highly competitive agricultural production, particularly wheat.

The restructuring of the trading zones is a challenge of a completely different dimension: the integration of new players within the regional blocks will increase the population but, above all, the integration of the sector risks causing serious disturbances due to the importance of price differentials for agricultural products and the need for a restriction to operate in the agricultural and downstream sectors. This restructuring is therefore both a great opportunity in terms of supply and opportunities and a challenge in terms of competition.

At the global level, future negotiations are a key issue for the sector. The application of the latest agreements (minimum access of third country products to the regional market, conversion of variable import levies to customs duties, and reduction of subsidized exports) has posed serious difficulties for certain sectors of activity, particularly dairy products, flour, salt, and poultry. In the latter sector, some countries' exports increased by 21.4 percent, while the exports of others were limited to 8.9 percent.

Unanimous common positions appear here and there on the main lines of the world agricultural strategy. The three general principles are, respectively, the reference supported by regional models of agribusiness based on multifunctionality, respect for the essential elements of the position of several countries with a view to future multilateral trade negotiations, and the defence of intrazone preference. The objectives of the negotiations for rich countries are

- Protection for regional products whose reputation for quality is linked to a geographical indication;
- Maintaining the balance of the various agreements, especially for internal support. In general, direct aids are preferable to course support, especially since they can contribute to certain multifunctional agribusiness missions, especially rural development;
- Some countries are ready to negotiate a process of reducing export subsidies as concessions are balanced with other major agricultural powers (US, in particular). This is explicitly targeted at export credits and the provision of food aid, two important elements of the American strategy to get foreign markets;
- Maintaining the concepts of "green box" and "blue box" as categories of negotiations for certain countries. Sustaining direct

support that is not fully decoupled from income is desirable for some countries;
- The more explicit confirmation of the precautionary principle, in order to ensure the safety and quality of food products.

It is unfortunate that policy makers do not sufficiently take into account the concerns of the agribusiness sector. Institutional stances should be firmly set in multilateral negotiations, recognizing the specificities of food choices, while allowing food businesses to improve their competitiveness in international trade.

Nevertheless, the dangers are real: the signing of some agreements has had catastrophic consequences for the poultry sector, while the market was booming. While the London group has been in favor of rapprochement, the Cairns group refuses the agricultural protectionism of some countries and considers the dismantling of tariff protection (import levies) and export subsidies (refunds) as priorities: we should see the disappearance of agricultural subsidies which constitute an obstacle to the smooth running of international trade.

Note that agro-production is also at the core of new technologies. Here, it is not a question of drawing up a complete picture of the new technologies or of pretending to apprehend all the consequences of these in the field of the agro-production. Nevertheless, through two precise examples, it is possible to measure the real ones. Impacts for agribusiness, on the one hand, biotechnology, on the other hand, information and communication technologies.

The term biotechnology was used for the first time by Karl Ereky, a Hungarian engineer, to discuss the science and methods that make it possible, from raw materials, to produce products using living organisms. But it was with Watson and Crick's double-helix model that modern biotechnology was born, even though it only prolonged animal and plant breeding and the use of microorganisms for beer production, wine, cheese, and bread started for centuries.

Since then, biotechnology has been the subject of significant commercial development, particularly in the United States. Biology has played an essential role in the green revolution which has been characterized by an unprecedented increase in agricultural productivity: tomorrow, the challenge for agribusiness is to feed several billion human beings, in quantity and quality, it is therefore legitimate that biotechnologies (from molecular biology) have focused not only on health, chemistry, energy, and the environment but also on agribusiness and agro-production.

Given the time-to-market of ideas from the labs, hundreds of small and medium-sized biotech companies have flourished in the United States and, to a lesser extent, in other rich countries. These technologies, the developments focused mainly on plants (the situation for animals is less favorable to transgenesis) for technical and economic reasons: it is indeed quite easy to market on a large scale various species of transgenic plants (tomatoes, soya, maize, rape...). We do not want to go into detail on this issue in this chapter. We take note of the current deadlock that these biotechnologies encounter, after an exponential development of cultivated areas in GMOs and the explosion of the turnover of some companies.

Many errors have been made in the presentation of these new technologies: lack of information and transparency, lack of genuine public consultation, aggressive strategies on the part of some companies... The first generation of GMOs has been condemned. Does this mean that agribusiness and production industries must definitely do without this technology?

At the risk of shocking, it is desirable to answer in the negative. Firstly, the potential scope of biotechnology over a twenty-year horizon is extremely broad: it includes improvements in product quality (taste, conservation, etc.), adapting plants to difficult conditions (drought, salinity...), increased yields by increased fixation of nitrogen, resistance to diseases and pests (parasites, insects), the biodegradability of fertilizers and pesticides, increased reliability and speed in animal health diagnostics and more efficient vaccines, the ability to formally identify a product throughout the production chain (traceability), new techniques for transforming microorganisms for industrial use...

The scale of this progress is likely to engage agribusiness and the processing industry in a new green revolution.

In addition, there is a great danger for the entire contemporary production and industrial sector: this is the question of patents. Nearly half of the revenues of companies working on biotechnology are devoted to research and development. Thus, half of the value of this industry lies in its intellectual capital. In order to protect themselves from copying and to enhance their discoveries, researchers, especially in the United States, have multiplied in recent years the filing of patents in this sector of activity. However, by leaving some companies to file nearly three quarters of biotechnology patents, other countries may simply limit the availability of products and keep prices at unduly high levels.

The agricultural and food sector of some countries could be confronted in the years to come with a capital risk constituted by the strategy of certain multinationals, which aim at ensuring a monopoly situation, by the possession of patents (patents which sometimes concern the protection of a knowledge and not of an innovation as it should be). This multiplication of specific patents is even more worrying as the process of patentability in some countries is seven times more expensive than elsewhere (United States, Canada, etc.).

Also, the advent of new information and communication technologies naturally has important consequences for agribusiness. We focus here on the need for the agribusiness industries to exploit the new information and communication technologies and on the risk that these same technologies have for the industry. Agribusiness sector, particularly in the event of a health accident on a product.

Subject to the demands of the markets, agribusiness companies are forced to implement new forms of management, with the aim of improving the quality of their products and reducing their costs. These new devices make it necessary to widely circulate information using, especially computer networks.

The computerization of the agribusiness industries allows, within the company itself, to improve the organization. Similarly, the establishment and management of quality processes and certification (which are often large consumers of digitized information) will require, in the future, to develop and refine these new tools. The reinforcement of internal communications in the company (via email addresses), the operation of management services, the location of setting-up places ... require the implementation of a large number of microcomputers in networks.

Modernizing the management of the agribusiness industries is a challenge: 43% of agro-production companies accounting for 17% of total turnover are still in "traditional" management. The agribusiness industry should also, through computer networks such as the Internet, disseminate extensive information about its products and, where appropriate, sell them online. E-commerce and teleshopping could channel 15 percent of sales of agribusiness products.

The new information and communication technologies thus appear as an instrument at the service of the agribusiness sector, making it possible to better approach and more directly the consumer. The setting up of such tools could enable the agribusiness industries, for a significant part of their production, to save distribution costs, or even to avoid the distribution network, and to achieve a better balance with GMS (Grandes et Moyennes).

Finally, the agribusiness sector will increasingly need to know and integrate in its strategy the considerable amount of data relating to consumer purchases. Consumer profiles will have to be collected and analyzed more and more. The agribusiness industries will therefore face a major technological challenge to segment markets finer, identify niche markets, and quickly detect new consumer trends. This information will need to be passed up the production chain to supply tight markets with increased reliability, reduced response times and lower costs.

The challenge of mastering new information and communication technologies for the agribusiness industries is also noticeable from a totally different angle. Indeed, if the sector must know how to make the best use of this tool in the future, both upstream, downstream and within its organization to improve its services and products, and at a lower cost, it must also integrate it into its strategic thinking and its definition of potential risks.

In a globalized society, where food safety and quality are daily topical issues, the occurrence of a food problem on a product, the origin of this difficulty is accidental, fraudulent or even purely theoretical, can, within a few hours, cause the complete ruin of an agribusiness enterprise within a few days.

In this respect, certain events are symptomatic of this challenge: as food controls are reinforced, in a heterogeneous global scientific and legal environment, the discovery of traces of listeria (traces that have not been confirmed by later controls) led to the commercial fall of a cheese whose brand was famous. In this case, the survival of the undertaking concerned comes exclusively from its integration into a large group. If this company had been independent, it would no longer exist. Such experience testifies to the capital challenge posed by the advent of new information and communication technologies.

To add to these scenarios, a consumer with a demanding trend. The notions of food safety and quality, the consideration of health in food, respect for environmental standards in production are certainly not new concepts. Nevertheless, the situation in this area has evolved. Indeed, if food is still a pleasure, the concerns of health, dietetics, or energy have changed from the consumer, in genuine requirements of authenticity and especially transparency in the manufacturing process.

In this respect, some lessons can be drawn from recent crises in the food sector. Crisis of chickens with dioxin, use of sewage sludge in the manufacture of animal feed, case of listeria, traces of salmonella, beef blood in the wines, the list is long of the crises occurred in the sector of the food. From fraudulent origin, accidental or simple unverified information, food security has been the "front page" of all daily and weekly newspapers. Added to this are the consumer's great fears about beef with hormones and genetically modified organisms. All this is sometimes a bit confusing in the mind of the consumer, even in the journalist's words. But what does it matter since the question that burns the lips is the same: is contemporary food safe?

Agribusiness will have to respond quickly to this question without any detour, or suffer disastrous consequences. As a result, the 27 percent of agribusinesses that apply international benchmarks of the ISO type seem very modest in terms of the food security issue.

The agribusiness industries will, tomorrow, establish perfect traceability at all stages of manufacture because once a link is missing, the entire system collapses. This imperative is financially burdensome, especially in a very heterogeneous economic, social, and regulatory environment. But no other way out is possible. Public authorities will have to actively participate in this priority strategy of food security: the creation of structures, the initiative of economic intelligence in some countries perfectly corresponds to the mission, which falls to the public authorities.

This imperative of food safety, in a context of suspicion, doubles, more and more, of a demand for products of quality. Some countries have many strengths in this area, with the signs of quality that will be the subject, tomorrow, of increased demand from consumers, especially in international markets. According to a recent poll, 66 percent of Americans would change brands for another labeled. The promotion of the quality of agribusiness products passes in the most by countries, in particular by that of the products of the terroirs.

The safety and quality of these products considered "typical," with a strong cultural connotation, will in the future be totally irreproachable: indeed, if an incident on a standard product is devastating for a company, the same problem on a product bearing a label or designation of origin could be catastrophic, not only for the company concerned, but also for the image of all food in a region or country.

Finally, the consumer is just starting to consider compliance with environmental standards. Today, agro-production invests an average of five hundred million dollars per rich country per year in water treatment, finances 65 percent of the budget of ecopackaging and devotes six hundred million dollars for tools to manage environmental protection. These efforts are clearly insufficient. Agribusiness has a serious delay in certification (international standard on environmental management) compared to partners.

However, this adaptation to environmental standards will become a priority in the future, at all levels of processing; the agribusiness company must ensure that the raw materials delivered to it comply with certain environmental standards: the development of agribusiness so-called "reasoned" with, for example, the green component "agricultural-confidence" set up by the agricultural cooperation of some countries, corresponds to this concern, but is still too limited.

In product processing, agro-production will have to comply with increasingly stringent environmental regulations regarding discharges (organic matter, production waste, water or sludge discharges, packaging waste, etc.). For example, the challenge of managing water for the sector in the future. Indeed, agribusiness consumes a large quantity of water for washing, extraction, cooking or for cooling, needs a decent quality water for the hygiene and taste quality of products, and leads to releases containing almost exclusively organic products.

Finally, the processed product will have to meet certain special characteristics (packaging...) so, again, to meet the requirements of consumers.

This consideration of environmental requirements will be accompanied, within animal chains, by an increased demand in terms of well-being: the consumer accepts less and less the intensive breeding (the recent regulation in some countries on the laying hens is one example), is increasingly interested in the conditions of animal transport and the methods of slaughter. The cattle or poultry production company that would not take these concerns into account tomorrow could be quickly blamed by the media and suffer the effects.

The consumer demands for safety, food quality, environmental, and animal welfare are legitimate. But it should also highlight the difficulties, of a sector that still suffers from a cruel lack of harmonization of food legislation and in a globalized world where the various national regulations are often far removed from real expectations, it will be necessary to act without delay: a difficult step.

While the establishment of a safe, high-quality agribusiness industry, which respects environmental measures and animal welfare, is now an imperative, it faces two major difficulties: first, regulatory harmonization in the food sector is still far from perfect. Admittedly, in the battle for the conquest (or preservation) of regional market shares, the agribusiness industry in some industrialized countries benefits from an image of quality conferred on it by its particularly sophisticated food identification system. Other systems prefer, on the contrary, the trademark and the labeling. While on this point, the regulation has progressed significantly with the introduction of protected designations of origin and protected geographical indicators, the harmonization of global strategies remains insufficient. Since the principle of mutual recognition of national rules in the field, several approaches come together. The minimalist, hygienist approach, which limits the harmonization of strategies to the definition of essential safety and information requirements, is based on the condition that labeling standards are sufficient to ensure protection and consumer information and the fairness of transactions.

This simplifying approach (a consumer spends about one second on the act of purchasing a food product), which is inconsistent with some of the objectives set out in the framework of harmonization strategies, not only puts the danger of adoption of the least stringent standards at the international level (which is the case for the definition of biological regulation in animal production) but still totally distorts the game of competition within the intrazone in many parts of the world, such as for example, for animal feed.

In addition to the difficulties of rich countries to define a coherent food law despite the creation of Consumer Directorate General and numerous declarations of intent, progress is needed in the application of labeling rules, especially for GMOs, in the implementation of adapted animal feed legislation, in the management of controls...

Paradoxically, next to whole sections, little or not considered by the standards of regulation, exists an excessive number of regulations, difficult to apply (a hundred or so directives).

Thus, the complexity and rigidity of the regulatory environment in rich countries undermine the ability of the agribusiness industry to anticipate and adapt to new international constraints. There is too much fragmentation and lack of coordination between the different countries in the development of measures concerning food safety and consumer protection.

This regulatory diversity in the field of food is even more important at the international level. Despite the conclusion of many agreements, the heterogeneity of legislation creates very strong distortions of competition that particularly affect Western agribusiness industries. The industrialized production sector will increasingly be faced at the international level with two approaches.

The first is the almost total absence of regulation for certain countries in the food sector or, on the contrary, the existence of extremely complex legislation. In the context of trade with these countries, industrialized agro-production will either have to deal with imports of food products at very low costs (and thus be tempted to relocate to these regions), or guard against protectionist temptations, from these countries.

In the face of this insufficiency or excess of regulation which is detrimental to world trade in a very sensitive sector, a second trend encourages the establishment of a real multilateral regulation. The creation of the World Trade Organization responds to this logic. Agreements on sanitary and phytosanitary barriers, technical barriers to trade and intellectual property rights have been designed with a dual purpose: to encourage the use of international standards and to guard against regulatory protectionism.

The development of international food standards is carried out within specific institutional structures. The normative work of these institutions is a challenge for the agribusiness sector. These international organizations, whose mission is to develop standards for agribusiness products, are to be commended. These bodies study and propose standards, codes, documentary texts that can be used as references in the global marketing of foodstuffs.

These standards will gradually be imposed to give a sound basis (at least hopefully) to the development of international trade. The appropriate organizations have, moreover, entrusted its structures with important missions which consist in eliminating, on an objective basis accepted by all, the technical obstacles to international trade.

This structuring, if it sometimes encounters operating difficulties, will see its role strengthened in the future. The countries concerned must have a strong presence not only as member countries submitting their own knowledge and experience in the scientific, regulatory, and industrial fields for the protection of consumers but also as responsible for committees of general principles to which the problems raised by the commissions to offer acceptable solutions. Because the norms are opposable in practice to the different countries, whether or not the latter have decided to accept them and incorporate them into their national regulations, the role of the experts in these bodies is strengthened in all areas, particularly, very important for the agribusiness sector, technological issues, and their relationship to the quality and authenticity of food.

Thus, for example, in order to ensure the correct application of certain agreements, the scientific basis is mandatory, the decision to be made on the basis of the risk analysis which includes risk assessment and management, as well as the risk communication.

The example of raw milk cheese is particularly revealing of the importance of these agencies in setting standards and rules applicable not only at the international level, but also at the level of national or regional regulations.

The industrialized agro-production industry must therefore, in the face of this institution, be very active in defining objectives and preparing dossiers. It must also participate in various regulatory bodies. The challenge of defining tomorrow's food standards and increasing consideration of "legitimate nonscientific factors" (consumer wishes, food tradition, etc.) within these bodies require the greatest vigilance of professionals and public authorities.

In addition, convinced of the need to change the relationship between, on the one hand, the commissions composed of several countries and, on the other hand, the management committees on sanitary and phytosanitary measures, and on technical barriers to trade.

CHAPTER 9

AGRIBUSINESS NEW REVOLUTION

To survive in this new globalized food order in which the consumer will increasingly succeed in making its individual demands prevail, where new technologies will be ubiquitous, agribusiness industries will have to make profound changes. To think that the only obtaining of an ISO qualification or any other, the maintenance of the export turnover, and the conclusion of partnerships with the large distribution via the development of the private brands, could be enough for the sector to face the challenges of international competition, the upheavals of consumption patterns, the imperatives of quality and safety ... would be a decoy.

Of course, it will be up to each company to define its industrial strategy. But the transformations in progress explain a change of mentality, of behavior of all the actors of the sector of the production as well as strategies. It is no longer a matter of constraining the upstream while undergoing the downstream, but of creating a real value chain. It is no longer a matter of remaining isolated in its internal market or devoting its development exclusively to exports, but, on the contrary, of winning back the national markets in order to be more successful in regional and international markets.

It is no longer a question of ensuring greater food safety and the minimum of quality of products, but of achieving a balance between excellence in quality and safety for the benefit of the consumer. It is no longer a question of spending a minimum of turnover on staff training and research and development, but to consider that these investments are the two priorities of the agro-production sector. It is no longer a matter for the public authorities to be either spectators or actors in industrial strategies, but to become a real arbiter who is both respectful of the rules and able to establish a permanent dialogue with the industrial sector. These are the conditions for the future of the agribusiness productive industry.

From this point of view, the industrialized agro-production industry must manage to evolve in a nonconfrontational environment (both upstream and downstream) if it wants to fully exploit its assets. The establishment of a spirit of industry must allow it to focus on its issues.

The agribusiness sector often regrets the fragmentation of supply and sometimes finds it difficult to find products that meet its requirements.

While understanding the difficulties faced by producers, and by supporting them in most of their efforts, there is a strong need for an organization of production and the different sectors. It is not normal that we fall back on "good years" and that we call to national solidarity the "bad."

Whatever the judgement on the organization of production, it is today an imperative both for the agricultural world and for agribusiness: in the face of strong groupings, the relationship between the agribusiness upstream will be required to rebalance. The example of certain industrialized countries proves it.

In addition, the generalization of a contractual strategy between industries and producers as well as the presence of a powerful cooperative sector (in which specific contracting methods are put in place with producers), should make it possible to strengthen the partnership. Between the agricultural world and that of agro-production.

The first two links in the food chain are made by the farmer and the industrialist, the latter transforming 70 percent of the overall production of the former.

The two partners therefore have every interest in cooperating, strengthening their links: weakening one of the two links is weakening the entire chain, and therefore its own structure.

This strategy is equally valid for industrial relations with distribution. The constant dialogue with the distribution becomes a real necessity.

Thus, the increasing sophistication of industrial processes, the growing importance of information gathering and analysis, research and development, and communication, are likely to increase fixed costs at all levels of the industry of agro-production.

Operating in more segmented markets, companies will face more and more risks. This parallel rise in costs and risks should reinforce the concern for the agribusiness industries to reach a critical size: nevertheless, this concentration will have difficulty reaching that of the supermarket.

Therefore, one of the key features of organizing the agro-production sector in the future may be to strengthen vertical relationships, particularly towards distribution. The segmentation of consumption should lead to a multiplication of slots and, thus, impose a tightening of the links between the different stages of the sector: indeed, the vertical coordination between the agro-production and its downstream should offer him a guarantee of outlets and, possibly a hedge against the risks of price variation.

However, the relations between these two actors were often unsuccessful, the mass retail being accused of exercising permanent domination.

Aware that cooperation cannot be decreed, even legislative measures will not succeed in stopping the domination of SMG in the food sector. The latest forecasts indicate that while, in theory, all links in the food chain seem to benefit from vertical coordination, in practice, relationships often move in favor of distribution.

Indeed, in a sector where information on demand is destined to become the "nerve of war," proximity to consumers is and could be a decisive asset for distribution companies. They would thus, more and more, have a "natural vocation" to organize the vertical relations and to influence the decisions of production and transformation, having the means to direct in their favor the sharing of the risks and the profits.

Policy makers should encourage economic strategies to organize, on the one hand, round tables between the various partners of the sector and, on the other hand, the basis of distribution in a systematic way. Beyond a necessary reorientation of the industrial strategy of the agro-production sector in the direction of a better response to demand, based on technological innovation and likely to impose brand awareness, only a change in the mindset of the "big" retailers could help rebalance the balance of power and evolve in a less confrontational environment, similar to what is already happening in some Western countries (the United States, in Great Britain, or Northern Europe).

It would be essential to estimate, for example, that these two actors share, equitably, the results of the optimization of the logistic relations.

It will also be necessary to worry about the interest that can induce, in the years to come, the development of sales of agricultural and processed products via, for instance, the Internet network. By having a direct contact with the consumer, the entrepreneur will be able to do without the distribution network. It is estimated that these sales channels will account for about 20 percent of total agribusiness sales in the coming years. Such opportunities would undoubtedly allow the agro-production sector to strengthen its weight in the food chain, especially with regard to supermarkets.

In addition, the initiatives of the cooperative sector should be approved, on the one hand, to improve emergency procedures in case of conflict, and on the other hand, to create a public body which would be given the task of ensuring that existing avenues of law against abuses of purchasing power is fully utilized.

The future of the agribusiness industries also passes by a strong adaptation of the industrial tool in the broad sense, that is to say including not only research and innovation, but also the financing capacities of agro-production as well as the Human Resource Management. In this sense, it will be necessary to engage in a more active research and innovation strategy.

The role of research would be to prepare for the future by mastering new technologies so that, in the food sector, it is possible to provide food with sufficient protein and carbon chains.

This research will lead to many innovations in agro-production, to allow the sector to maintain its market share and to gain new ones. The strengthening of research and innovation therefore seems essential in the industrialized agribusiness to face on a level playing field with competitors, contemporary food challenges in both industrialized and developing countries.

There are many cases of inadequate private research in the agribusiness industry: the figures vary widely but average 0–9 percent of industry added value. By adding public funding for the civil budget for research and technological development in some countries, which includes institutional grants to major research institutions, official resources and public funds reached the overall figure of 1.5 percent.

This average is to be compared with that of all industrial enterprises in developed countries, where private research accounts for almost 3 percent on average of added value. Private sector research is almost four times lower than that of industry as a whole, making agribusiness the industry's "red lantern" for research.

Admittedly, this observation varies greatly depending on the sectors (like that of seeds) and companies. For example, some firms spend up to 12 percent of their turnover on research. Nevertheless, in recent years, research in agro-production has remained largely inadequate: were not there only about 1000 public researchers and an average of 1300 private researchers in the sector? Research and development in the production sector employs fewer than three thousand people on average, which is only twice the amount of public research workers now working in the food sector in industrialized countries.

In the United States, the Bayh-Dole Act (a law on patents) has given research institutions the right to become owners of patents resulting from innovations from their laboratories that have benefited from public subsidies. This device liberalizes the previous system, which wanted only the public power to be able to own these patents, and attracts a growing group of researchers from all countries that see their work valued: in a few years, the number of universities making efforts to transfer technology has increased tenfold.

The United States expects to increase these devices in the coming years because of their lack of engineers (there are 5.4 of young graduates in the United States for eighteen, 5 percent in other rich countries). The other industrialized countries will thus have to avoid a new brain drain, the specialists of valorization, in particular in the agribusiness, being in insufficient number according to most of the experts.

Nevertheless, the challenge for research in agro-production is both quantitative and qualitative. The opposition between food tradition and technological innovation must thus be overcome. Researchers must simultaneously explore these two concepts in order to identify new fields of investigation.

In addition, researchers need to get closer to the economic world, to listen to concerns and translate them into research programs, and transfer their knowledge in all areas to control the quality of products: physical process modeling, chemical and biological agribusiness industry, development of analytical methods, development of sensors, and transformation processes, etc.

The public authorities must support these research efforts by multiplying the multi-year interdepartmental programs: these programs have set themselves the goal of strengthening the links of industry with public research, in the fields of food industrial engineering, biotechnology, quality, nutrition, and toxicology.

The initiative of scientific research interest groups for the food industry in certain countries, which brings together scientists from several specialized research organizations and whose objectives are to improve consultation on research in agro-production, is an example to follow.

The cure for the various malfunctions in agribusiness research in some countries is less a question of financial means than of coordination and rationalization of existing organizations and mechanisms.

The agribusiness industries, which have become "high-tech" industries, confronted with ever more complex sectors, the explosion of scientific knowledge, and the increased demands of consumers, are doomed to meet the challenge of research: a start is necessary to the share of industrialists and financiers as well as public authorities.

One of the explanations put forward to justify the low level of research and development expenditure is the importance of sums committed to innovation and products, which includes the study of consumer expectations, the analysis of needs, the design, marketing.... Product innovation allows, for example, a food industry to increase its growth by creating added value, a challenger to get closer to the leader of a market....

In some cases, product innovation results in the launch of an average of 1500 references each year, a figure that increases annually from 10 to 15 percent.

Product innovation requires significant resources: thus, the budget for launching a product by a major national brand is from 0.76 to 3.56 million dollars for advertising, 5 million on average millions dollar for industrial investment, 1 million dollars on average for SEO, 0.5 million dollars on average marketing studies and about an average of 1 million dollars per country for research, development and testing.

Nevertheless, the success is very uncertain: in fact, about five hundred ideas, fifty concepts emerge and only six technical-marketing studies are started on average overall by country. Finally, on two products launched, only one new product succeeds. Of these successful new products, only 30 percent survive after two years. We must be aware that it is much more difficult to stimulate or create consumer cravings in the field of agro-production (already widely explored) than in computer products or Wi-Fi. In nine out of ten cases, it is not the research and development teams that are behind the innovation, but the marketing that has become essential with the advent of supermarkets and brand development.

Given the evolution of the agro-production sector, the novelty of the product will have to give the way to more added value, such as nutrition and especially safety.

If large groups are forced to innovate, small- and medium-sized enterprises as well as small- and medium-sized industries are not left out. Nevertheless, because of the small sums that it can devote to product innovation, it is desirable that the tools made available to the technical support centers for agribusiness industries be developed.

After the useful reorganization in some countries of associations of technical centers for the agribusiness industry, these technical centers must continue to pool their efforts in order to usefully establish partnerships with their foreign counterparts, which are often much larger in size.

In addition, the networking of professional technical centers in other countries, which have a vocation of national action on a profession, regional centers that provide small- and medium-sized enterprises with very close support and generic technical centers that are specialized in a given technique, must be emphasized. Small- and medium-sized businesses will be able to find, within a hundred kilometres of their locations, the analysis and information services they need for their analysis and development, which they often lack.

In addition, it is advisable to study the possibility for the technical centers of agro-production to acquire own funds in order to be able to mobilize rapidly capital for small and medium industries as well as small- and medium-sized enterprises.

Moreover, we should advocate an evolution of the research tax credit, like the Quebec system: in order to keep this system highly incentivized, and without questioning all the procedures, the establishment of a new basis of calculation (added value or total expenditure on research, for example) and modulated rates could encourage companies to involve scientific and technical partners in their innovation initiatives.

Similarly, the introduction of favorable tax incentives for individuals to invest in innovative firms, such as in the United States, would be a valuable tool for developing research in the industrialized world.

Standards on innovation and research in different countries may be particularly interesting in agribusiness. First, these standards offer public researchers the opportunity to retain their status for a certain period of time as they create "a small- and medium-sized industry or small- and medium-sized enterprise of the future." Second, the installation of an incubator (public research organization) allows small businesses to benefit from various services (premises, equipment...) which constitute savings.

Also, managing dynamically employment, an essential component of the development of the agro-production sector, becomes a necessity. The image of the sector, in the social field, is contrasted. On the one hand, agribusiness industries are the third largest employer in the industry of rich countries, with 10 percent of industrial employment. Employment has, moreover, resisted in this industrial branch rather than in others during the past years. In addition, in recent years, the agribusiness industries have created net new jobs, with an average of more than 5,000 jobs per country. Finally, from the beginning, there has been an increase in the qualifications of positions.

On the other hand, agro-production is characterized by a relatively low staffing rate and a lower level of qualification than other industrial sectors (the workers' share being 61 percent, compared to an average of 37 percent). A small percentage of young people, and underdeveloped vocational training with expenditures of 2.5 percent of the wage bill (as against 3.2 percent) on average in economy. In addition, agribusiness industry trades suffer from a bad image and have a reputation for offering difficult working conditions (as one of the areas where people work the most at night and on weekends). End.

Several tools have been put in place for training in this sector for a number of years and depending on the country, such as, for example, prospective study contracts, the training insurance fund, and tripartite on vocational training. Nevertheless, it is imperative, in order to face new challenges, to take much more into account for the issues of vocational training.

Public authorities in this area must play a dynamic role by encouraging, in particular, the smallest companies to invest in the training of their staff. The reluctance of the administration to renew for the third time the agreement for the agribusiness industries on the commitment to development of training, which had been a real success, appears, in this respect, regrettable.

In addition, the improvement of working conditions in certain sectors is essential.

Another major issue is whether to reduce the working time in the production sector. In terms of reducing the length of working time, it is necessary to recall several obvious facts: firstly, all legislation must take into account the specificities of each sector: thus, in certain sectors, dressing and undressing times exceed three hours a week due to hygiene standards. Should all of these hours be charged to working time?

In addition, some companies rely heavily on fixed-term contracts because of the seasonality of their activity, often in full agreement with employees. Should we strictly prevent such practices, without distinguishing the necessary fight against the precariousness of work from the good functioning of companies that made the effort to negotiate with their employees on legal and consensual basis?

On the other hand, any strengthening of social legislation in a country (in the same way as in the field of the environment, food safety and even legitimate food quality) often reinforces the competitive situation of partners and third countries by increasing distortions of competition.

Also, real financing capacities should be identified: agribusiness companies have to face growing investment needs, particularly in the face of the explosion of advertising expenditure, which is almost twice that of material investments estimated at about twenty billion on average per year. This sector is also characterized by low profitability, insufficient equity, an added value of 18 percent of turnover compared to 30 percent on average in other industries and a gross operating surplus of the order of 7.8 percent against 9–10 percent in the rest of the industry.

With an average of fewer than 5 percent, the self-financing generated does not adequately cover the investment charge, leading to significant indebtedness.

In addition, the ratio of indebtedness to equity is 5 percent of points higher than the industry average and the weight of equity in the balance sheet total is only 20 percent.

This weakness is due to the structure of the industrial fabric in the different countries (small- and medium-sized companies represent more than 60 percent of the turnover of the branch in certain cases) but also to the insufficiency of capitalization of the results.

For a banker, on a scale of risks, the agribusiness industries belong to the category of "mature sectors," moderately exposed with a default rate of 1.5 percent, which is twice as low as other sectors. Nevertheless, agro-production has a significant sensitivity to cyclical crises, even more so because it is close to the upstream and its products are less processed. In addition, the difficulty in finding a partner in equity lies in the fact that the growth of the agribusiness activity is relatively weak in the short term and hardly releases a good valuation of the invested capital.

For example, in some countries, production cooperatives which are linked to the territory both by their members and the contribution of their capital on the one hand, by the nature of their activities and the origin of their raw material, somewhere else.

In view of the financial needs necessary for the development of enterprises in the cooperative sector, two measures are desirable: firstly, the rapid introduction (this measure is included in the agricultural regulations of certain countries) of the extension of the provision for investments in the shares of the cooperative, when these constitute the counterpart of capital financing the new investments.

In addition, it is necessary to encourage the establishment of instruments intended to drain the savings of producers, members of cooperatives, or suppliers of agribusiness industries. This tool, the agricultural enterprise savings plan in some countries, would strengthen upstream-downstream links, increase the company's own funds, and would be a lever for raising capital.

These arrangements should be accompanied by a tax advantage (tax exemption linked to the blocking of savings). The tax incentive is an interesting element that will not be decisive in the agricultural world. It follows that the feasibility of the product should not be studied from the point of view of taxation, but also from an industrial and financial point of view. Whatever the design of the product, it can only be used by companies that generate a minimum of profitability.

Secondly, the need to resort to external financing must be considered. The systematic use of self-financing may, in the long run, be a brake on the development of agribusiness industries. In such circumstances, it is desirable to encourage the multiplication of partnerships between agro-production and the banking system, which are still too inadequate. Similarly, the development of the IPO (less than 1 percent of the total average agribusiness industries are listed) and that of financial bodies specializing in venture capital is imperative, especially for small- and medium-sized enterprises.

In this respect, the public authorities have a decisive role to play: there are many types of financing depending on the country (funds, grants, etc.) but they are too often overlooked. It is true that the erosion of agricultural orientation premiums for years is hardly encouraging. In a large majority of cases, the steady and steady decline in industrial strategy credits, which represent just 0.2 percent of the budgets of the responsible institutions. This is even more damaging since the reforms of the various sectoral strategies (depending on the country), by reducing the guarantee and price support mechanisms, have often transferred to industries, an increased responsibility for the valorization of agricultural productions.

It is important to note that local communities by countries are increasingly being called by the bedside of companies. If they cannot and must not substitute for the choice of the company, the local partners will nonetheless play a growing role in favor of agribusiness industries located in their territory. The information of the agribusiness industries on all the devices at their disposal is, moreover, a necessity.

In this configuration, it is essential to put the consumer at the center of the global food strategy.

The primacy given to food safety, food quality, and the environment in agro-production appears to be a legitimate and irreversible requirement. Nevertheless, it leads to an obvious additional cost for the agro-production sector. Thus, it is imperative that these objectives can be imposed not only on countries but also on regional configurations and at the international level. Ignoring this aspect would simply condemn this sector of activity in the medium term.

Dialogue is thus necessary and transparent between all the actors of food.

The consideration of food safety, the development of a real quality strategy, and the integration of the environment in any industrial strategy require not only the involvement of agro-production professionals, independent certification bodies, but also and above all public authorities: the cooperation of all these actors must lead to a permanent dialogue. The recent food crises have demonstrated the adverse effects of a confrontation between industry and the public authorities, or even within the public authorities. Joint crisis management is a necessity.

New institutional organizations, including the creation of industrial strategy and production services, perfectly match this partnership approach. While governments have full responsibility for developing regulations, controls and possible sanctions, agribusinesses are able to put in place food safety and quality processes that are validated and controlled by the government.

This dialogue should create a spirit of cooperation that will prove even more effective in food incidents. These can be better analyzed, better managed, and provided with information that is both transparent and objective. It is not a question of setting up a system that would keep the consumer away: this time is largely over. But the dissemination of false information is as detrimental to the company and the employees as to the consumer, who has no benchmark.

The ongoing dialogue between scientists, experts, professionals, consumers and government representatives on emerging societal issues, particularly in the area of new technologies, should be kept constant. This dialogue could involve partnerships with specific organizations.

In addition, it would be desirable for regional economic and social councils to take up the subject of biotechnology, in order to analyze and explain it objectively in each case: this decentralization of the consensus would allow everyone to learn to get involved and give your opinion on this delicate question. The biotech industry has freed itself from democratic rules: the sanction was up to the error. It is now imperative to renew the dialogue.

Finally, it is urgent to put in place measures that make it possible to substitute fossil carbon (oil) for agricultural carbon in many areas (lubricants, detergents, chemical solvents, cosmetics, etc.). These measures would, on the one hand, lead to a significant increase in industrial outlets for agricultural products and, on the other hand, would constitute a new way of presenting in a very different way the interest of biotechnologies, particularly with regard to public opinion.

While agribusiness exchanges take place, for more than two thirds in the intrazone, food must become "priorities for the major regions of the world," particularly with regard to health security. The creation of independent regional food agencies could be one of the strategic food security options that supranational institutions need to anticipate. In addition, it is necessary to define, as soon as possible, the concepts of precautionary principle in order to apply them carefully.

We must be aware of the imperative need of the precautionary principle, which requires, when it is implemented, that the actors involved must as soon as possible prove the safety of the products concerned for the health of consumers. Nevertheless, if the content and modalities of this principle were not to be more clearly defined, the industrialized world could be confronted in the coming times with excessively heavy litigation.

Indeed, the cost to a company of contamination or a presumption of contamination can be several million for a "small disaster" and hundreds of millions of dollars for a major accident. To this must be added the loss of consumer confidence in this product.

In such a context, regulatory authorities must ensure the appropriateness of their measures, because in the event of harm related to the triggering of an alert by inexact suspicion of a hazard, companies could ask to be compensated.

It should then be noted the importance of the three corollary principles of the precautionary principle: proportionality, compensation and adaptation. The first principle requires respect for a proportionality between the harm suffered by the community and the precautionary measure taken with regard to the company (withdrawal of lots, important information on the media, etc.). The second principle requires, in the event of a serious error of analysis by the supervisory authorities vis-à-vis the company, the compensation for the damage suffered, at least financially.

In fact, the damage done to a food brand can lead to its disappearance, a phenomenon that is difficult to evaluate precisely. Finally, the third principle recognizes the sometimes nonpermanent nature of the rules put in place in the name of the precautionary principle, which must be able to adapt to a new environment.

The discovery of certain facts, the analysis of scientific data and the regularization of particular situations may lead to the lifting of measures that have been imposed in the past. The precautionary principle is not intended to apply permanently, it must be able to adapt to changes in the environment.

It is difficult to explain to the public a change in health strategy, especially in the field of food. Nevertheless, if the measures taken in the name of the precautionary principle become permanent without taking into account changes after the outbreak of this principle, it may be emptied of its substance and become a general principle of suspicion.

The meaning and scope of the precautionary principle should be clarified in terms of current international law, the potential consequences for the development of science and its applications, and the impact on liability regimes.

It also seems essential for intraregional governments to simplify and modernize their food legislation and to develop homogeneous regulations. Recently, for example, representatives of meat industry professionals have been unable to agree on mandatory labeling around the world.

However, this failure does not come from purely technical considerations: some countries have issued the possibility of abandoning traceability and, in any case, refuse it to be mandatory. While others are needed, such as labeling on beef (a costly operation to ensure traceability), many of the professionals (supported by their country) refuse to apply this principle. While others tag, their manufacturers gain market share, competitiveness gains being real.

Although the first steps have been taken by the regulatory institutions, much remains to be done to put the consumer at the center of the industrialized countries' food strategy.

Thus, in the context of the growing internationalization of agribusiness trade and production, considering consumer requirements in terms of food safety and quality as well as the environment is a major imperative not only for consumers themselves but also for the food industry. Indeed, the proliferation of these standards has an increasing cost for the global agribusiness sector.

In terms of market access, growth in world trade in agricultural products and agribusiness output has averaged 5 percent in recent years per year, reaching almost six hundred billion dollars today. While developed countries have kept their commitments to open tariff quotas, the evolution of world market shares shows that the liberalization of agricultural markets has mainly benefited some developing countries: Western Europe has lost 4.3 percent market share and North America 0.7 percent to Latin America (plus 2.3) and Asia (plus 2.2) shares of Africa, Middle East and Central Europe remain constant. For some countries in particular, this decline is particularly significant in cereals and dairy products.

It is in this context that the integrated agenda requires reopening from new agribusiness and service trade discussions. A given number of countries also wish to continue to deal with "traditional" industrial trade issues (tariffs, technical barriers to trade). Key "new topics" should be introduced as they increasingly appear as elements of the global competitiveness of the powers (environmental standards, social standards, competition law, industrial property, investment rules).

That is why the Western countries, and more particularly some countries, argue for a broad round of negotiations. The United States, on the contrary, makes these integrated agendas the top priority of the next round of multilateral trade negotiations, to which would add discussions on limited industrial tariffs to a few targeted sectors.

Globalization appears as a reality to which the agro-production chain cannot escape, but which calls for vigilance concerning the rules of the game: it is at this price that the opening of economies can be a source of growth and employment.

In addition, the forthcoming negotiations should end with a single undertaking. This implies that in the absence of a global agreement on all the defined sectors; countries do not accept a separate agreement. If the notion of "early harvests" (that is, the obtaining of results on certain subjects) advanced by the Americans cannot be ruled out on consensual themes, it would be necessary to refuse certain sectors, such as the agribusiness, fisheries or agro-production, to be considered as a "bargaining chip" and to be the subject of specific agreements, as it was the case in the past.

It is also important to ensure a balance between the markets. In this respect, the contribution of the agribusiness sector to the trade surplus of the developed countries is a reality, particularly for a number of countries. Nevertheless, the development of the agribusiness industries requires not only the consolidation of its positions on the Community markets but also the conquest of emerging markets and the preservation of the internal market.

Since an agro-production company has managed, at the cost of major efforts, to capture an external market, it is often tempted to develop its trade first on this new market.

However, international crises, particularly in Russia and Asia, are sometimes indicative of a bad geographical position. In fact, wanting to export too much, the agribusiness industries must not turn away from their internal markets. This relative lack of interest in the internal market is not exclusive to large groups, even though small- and medium-sized enterprises/small- and medium-sized industries, scattered over all national territories, are often more focused on their regional markets than export.

This problem concerns in fact, the entire industrial fabric of certain countries, the opening of regional markets having strongly encouraged a large number of companies near the borders to make a growing turnover in foreign markets. The majority of export-oriented companies confirm the importance for companies to sell a minimum amount of production in their internal markets, in order to be able to protect themselves from changes in the international situation and health safety problems. And, at the same time, supplying domestic markets at lower costs (especially logistically).

In this configuration, the consolidation of the different regional markets is necessary. In fact, industrialized agribusiness accounts for more than 70 percent of its exports to intrazone countries: this market is a major asset for the agribusiness industries, particularly because of the tariff rules. Without neglecting its basic agricultural production, some countries must strive to export highly valuable products that enhance the efforts of industrial branches. Recent statistics on trade and industrialized agro-production are worrying as the presence of different countries in their regional markets has slightly declined in recent years.

Indeed, while trade balances with some of the leading agribusiness partners in some countries are in surplus, they have experienced a slight decline for some time. In addition, the deficit with a number of countries is growing significantly since it exceeds 1.52 billion dollars.

The balance with others, after having experienced a very strong progression, has continued to erode to fall to 60.90 million on average by developed countries and leave room for a deficit of several million agribusinesses must absolutely boost their exports in the regional markets, which are still a favorite zone, while taking advantage of opportunities in emerging markets.

For a long time now, the international market shares of agribusiness products of developed countries have been eroding slowly, but steadily: this decline comes from the arrival of new exporters of products such as Malaysia, Thailand....

Western exports of agribusiness industries to third countries (outside the zone) represent on average only 28.5 of total exports: Asia absorbs 20.5 percent of Western exports, the North and Central America, 8 percent, eastern countries, 12 percent the Near and Middle East, 11.5 percent, and North Africa and sub-Saharan Africa, each close to 10 percent. Finally, exports from some rich countries to the Mercosur countries account for fewer than 4 percent of total exports of agricultural products to third countries.

Certainly, the Russian and Asian crises have highlighted the dangers of researching "at any price" new markets outside the regional areas, as well as the fragility that would result from an excessive dependence of a small number of customers.

Nevertheless, in full force of a growing globalization of trade and facing the significant increase of the demand of emerging countries in the field of food, it is desirable for the agribusiness industries, to diversify their exchanges towards Asia (China and India), and from Latin America (Brazil, Argentina, Chile). It should be taken as an example of India which offers, through a local establishment, immense possibilities both in the dairy sector and in that of fruits and vegetables.

Moreover, it should not be forgotten that the export of agribusiness products is also the promotion of a food model. While large agribusiness companies often serve as the "locomotive" for such projects, small- and medium-sized enterprises/small- and medium-sized industries in different countries need to organize and create partnerships to conquer these difficult but promising markets.

CONCLUSION

The medium-term development prospects of the industrialized agro-production sector depend on its ability to respond to the challenges of a new global food order that has begun to emerge, but whose effects are still largely to come.

These industries will thus have to be perfectly integrated into the internationalization of trade, as well as to fulfil, inter alia, the requirements of the trilogy of safety, quality, and the environment.

Beyond the economic and industrial strategies mentioned in this book, the contemporary agribusiness sector should mobilize mechanisms to

- Foster, in close consultation with the professionals concerned, consumer organizations, scientists and public, and health and consumer decision makers, the establishment of charters on "sensitive" products (the most important of which is cheese from raw milk) in order to improve safety and to preserve, at the different international negotiations, food models;
- Submit motions for resolutions in the agricultural, forestry, and agribusiness sectors in view of the negotiations;
- To propose on the institutional credits for the projects dedicated to the production and agribusiness sector several budgetary measures, in order to consolidate and develop the sector;
- Finally, to elaborate norms allowing to transcribe in national law the international conventions to produce plant varieties.

These perspectives stem from the observation that the person pushing the cart confusedly perceives the complicated paths followed by the products he has purchased. He knows that an agricultural product is at the origin, that a farmer has necessarily been involved in its development. He also knows that in doing so, the farmer has changed the nature and the countryside. Often, he imagines a very close proximity between the work of the living done by many others and the very intimate act of eating to live, to eat to be healthy, to eat for to take pleasure in it. Yet, the relationship has distended.

On the other hand (most often an urban) he no longer understands what the producers really do: too many screens have emerged, too many uncertainties seem to have formed. It is difficult for him to understand the "discomfort" of the peasants, apparently poorly paid for their efforts, although they receive large subsidies in several countries.

It is also difficult for him to understand how these agricultural subsidies are an obstacle in international trade negotiations. While the distant provenance of certain products intrigues him or the poverty of the producers of the least developed countries can revolt him, the situation of the latter appearing morally unacceptable and strategically dangerous.

The increase in the population of the globe at the same time as the awareness of the finiteness of the resources worries him. And even more so because the responsibility of the man appears to him more and more obvious concerning the climatic disturbances, about which the unanimity is far from being acquired on the corrective means to be put in place.

But the awareness is growing: man is part of the biosphere and his actions become determinant on its durability and viability.

The historical period in which we have enrolled is between two original moments: the period when demographic acceleration was greatest and the period when the world population should reach its maximum.

Throughout this period, various resources will have been consumed to enable the lives of the greatest number. But we know that the adjustments, especially by the markets, have never been completely satisfactory since they have resulted and are still translated by intolerable results: many die of hunger and large populations suffer from food imbalances.

The global agribusiness system, and its related regional food systems, have been deformed and will still be transformed by humans.

Finally, the challenge is for men to remain in control of current and future transformations, so that they can better organize their lives in a system whose constraints are tightening more and more. Resources are geographically unequally distributed in relation to needs: the movement of commodities, goods, and people is a means of correcting the gaps between productive capacities and vital demands at the local level.

The margins of maneuvers are narrow, hence the importance of the rules on which men must agree, both globally and in every region of the globe. This is the object of all attempts at global and national corporate governance....

However, it is not possible to wait: we must act by dialing with initiatives already launched or bearing in mind the fixed deadlines. A glance of step when the time comes should make it possible to evaluate where the big distribution is. It would be appreciated that the most alarming forecasts, which estimate that Westerners would be two out of three to be threatened with obesity in the coming years, do not prove to be erroneous.

How to make each actor adopt the right attitude? A good understanding of sustainable development can be of effective universal help. It is therefore not to reduce this notion to the environment, as it is too often the case. It is also not to be fooled by the "commercial recovery" that can be made of this concept. Each actor would benefit from conforming his conduct to the real definition of sustainable development. Geographically, it is necessary to have a planetary conception; in terms of time, it is an intergenerational point of view that should be adopted.

In these conditions, sustainable development is at the crossroads of economic development, social progress, and respect for the environment: the three concerns must be simultaneous.

Thus, to speak of "sustainable economic development" is a sign that the notion of sustainable development has not been understood. Indeed, this consideration is partial, while the good attitude must be global: to be sustainable, development must necessarily be satisfactory on the economic level.

Let us remember: sustainable development is a development that is viable, liveable, and equitable. Viable, it is satisfactory from the environmental and economic points of view; liveable, it is satisfactory from the environmental and social points of view; fair, it is satisfactory from the social and economic points of view.

Adopting this attitude makes it possible to constantly correct current actions and calendars. The intensity of these changes suggested by all actors will result in conditions for everyone.

All actors, whoever they are, with more or less intensity, will seek to maximize their satisfaction from the point of view of food, health, environment, energy....

Obviously, the relative position of each will never correspond to the proposed utopia, leading to inevitable conflict situations. But it is clear that this attitude leads all actors, even those whose concern is not to make explicit their opinion, to "stimulate," ultimately, agribusiness.

On the other hand, those whose operational responsibilities are directly linked to food, health, nature, and energy must understand that they directly stimulate agribusiness. And if the connection may seem more diffuse for those who (as mere consumers) consider themselves the furthest away from the agricultural act, it is nonetheless real.

It is probably the business of decision makers to make all that is desirable for food, health, nature, and energy readable. To make it readable for all, and especially for those who are operationally responsible for the agribusiness act.

In these conditions of sustainable development, a truly offensive strategy, without taboos, can be set out to stimulate agribusiness, mechanisms specific to each country, regional mechanisms, and global mechanisms.

At all levels, it will regulate and frame behavior. The governance rules must be articulated between the different levels of action (UN, WTO, FAO, world regions, countries, etc.), so that the actors (very large multinational companies, many small and medium enterprises, many small businesses, countless consumers, countless taxpayers, countless citizens, etc.) can intelligently master globalization. Distributors, logisticians, processors, industrialists and artisans, producers (of food, health, nature, and energy), etc., are linked by powerful processes whose strategy must mark the meaning. The tremendous development of large-scale retailing, for example, can become, without the knowledge of more and more professional daily traders, a powerful pauperization diffuser. Where does the "cheaper than cheaper" lead? While all men are looking for more value.

Temporary protections in terms of economic strategies have been an excellent stimulus for agribusiness in some countries to meet regional objectives. Based on this success, conditions have fortunately been modified, so that strategies should be reinvented with new agricultural incentives, consistent with the desired regional development models, as well as with overall development, by prohibiting the implementation of places of mechanisms that would prove to be destructive assets.

At the same time, it seems necessary to take part in establishing the temporary protections that would be necessary for such "oases" to be formed in the least developed countries. It is their interest, but it is also that of the rich countries: the demographic, agricultural, energy, and ecological balances could be better controlled.

In the same way, it will be necessary to celebrate the progress of emerging countries, provided that it is done without dumping: economic, social, fiscal, and ecological.

Indeed, which informed consumers would agree to "eat deforestation from the Amazon" while savoring a 'cheaper" steak? Which African should agree to run out of rice while Southeast Asian rice is offered for sale on conditions that discourage production? And which Canadian citizen donating to a nongovernmental organization would not be disappointed when this same African is led to abandon the well that has just been drilled?

Agribusiness models can be stimulated. But they must be appropriate. And even more so because no one can seriously assure today that all men, and everywhere, will have the agribusiness resources they will need in the years to come.

As some say, "we need all agribusinesses." Including in countries, which are, at least during this period, under conditions of sufficient agricultural resources. Every effort must be made to forestall any more stringent changes that may occur later in the world. It will also surely and surely stimulate modern agribusiness, preserving and restoring the necessary fertility.

Also, research and innovation must be geared to improve the entire agribusiness system. In particular, it becomes clear that there is no point in contrasting "intensive" or "productive" agribusiness with respect for the environment: it is an "eco-intensive" agribusiness that we need.

We should say "eco-intensive" agribusiness preserves the existing "oases" and makes it possible to generate where men absolutely need it. These "oases" must be carefully preserved to make local life satisfactory. But we know that certain areas will no longer be able to achieve these goals without exchanges. This is the case of North Africa, etc.

Likewise, there is no more open than some together: no region of the world matters nor exports as much as them. Yet, their markets are "mature." Some countries in particular innovate, import, export, invest worldwide, and welcome investors from all over the world, including agro-production.

Although they may be threatened at the level of certain agricultural activities if the liberalization of the trade was done without taking into account the complexity of the realities of the living thing, they have relative interests determining. And especially if they are preserved with intelligence, without harming the constitution of similar sets in the world.

The path is probably narrow from a near planetary point of view, with the identified risks becoming more numerous. We must therefore find new parades while not sabotaging the existing devices, which protect us from erratic movements.

Similarly, if we are to innovate, because of some poorly known natural limits, the time is precisely for intensification of research to engage only reversible processes not likely to impoverish the unique biosphere.

On the other hand, if we put ourselves "here and now," the conditions are good for saying what we want as agribusiness models. Even producers are convinced that, to move forward, the reasoning should not be "centered agriculture": the fewer producers, the more agribusiness is everyone's business.

But let us know that it is not possible to approach this question of society without accepting to understand the complexity of the living which is at the base.

Our local, national, continental, or global institutions provide spaces where it is possible to build and negotiate the conditions for a better life between us. Nature, food, health, and energy: agribusiness models demand the attention of all, for the life and comfort of each and every one of us.

GLOSSARY

Absolute advantage: The advantage that a country has over many others for the production of certain goods or services, because of certain factors of production at its disposal — abundant arable land, favorable climate for agribusiness, or a highly skilled workforce for high-tech manufacturing activities. This means that it can produce certain goods or services at a lower cost than other countries, and it therefore clearly has an interest in specializing in the production and export of the goods and services in question. But even countries that do not have absolute benefits can benefit from international trade; see comparative advantage.

Accumulation of capital: Development of capital goods through investment.

Actual Indicator: Economic indicators based on prices of any base year. This approach takes into account fluctuations in market prices and thus makes it possible to bring out more clearly the other factors of economic change. For cross-country comparisons, this expression also applies to converting indicators calculated in local currency units into a common currency (the US dollar, for the most part). Actual indicators are calculated using the purchasing power parity (PPP) conversion factor, while the nominal indicators are those converted into dollars at current exchange rates.

Adventice: Adjective or noun designating a weed.

Adventitious organs: An organ in botany, appearing in a place "where it is not expected."

Adventive: Adjective qualifies the roots that appear on the stems or rhizomes.

Agricultural tractor: A self-propelled wheeled or tracked vehicle that performs towing functions of trailers or agricultural machinery with drawbars, accessories support, or machines installed either at the front or at the rear thanks to lifting arms, agricultural machinery animation comprising rotating parts or cylinders, through a PTO or a hydraulic system.

Agriculture: All the works transforming the natural environment for the production of plants and animals useful for humans.

Alpine pastures: A mountain pasture where cattle, sheep, or goat-herds are driven mainly in the summer.

Amendment: Provision of a product to improve soil quality (in terms of structure and acidity).

Ammo nitrate: Mineral nitrogen fertilizer based on ammonium nitrate.

Amortization: Decrease in the value of certain goods in order to consider their wear or obsolescence. Depreciation reduces a company's earnings, but does not constitute a cash outflow and therefore does not reduce a company's cash position.

Aquaculture: Generic term for all aquatic animal and plant production activities.

Arbitrage: An operation that consists of buying a good at a good price and reselling it simultaneously at a higher price to make an immediate profit. When the transaction is successful, no significant risk is incurred and a profit is derived from the transaction. A means of resolving a conflict other than through the courts.

Artificial insemination: In breeding, a technique that involves artificially fertilizing a female.

Asset: An asset is everything that belongs to you. It can be money that you hold in a checking or savings account, private property, investments, real estate, etc.

Auditor: An accountant who conducts audits to give an opinion on the fairness of the company's image given by its financial statements.

Authorized capital: The number of shares that a company is legally authorized to issue.

Balance sheets (statement of financial position): Financial statement that indicates the financial situation of a person, couple, family, company, etc. on a given date. It contains the list of its assets and liabilities, as well as its net worth (difference between assets and liabilities).

Bark: Protective outer covering of the trunk, branches, and roots of trees, and more generally woody plants.

Barn: Livestock buildings intended for the housing of cattle (cows, calves, etc.).

Beekeeping: Breeding bees for the production of honey.

Biennial: Adjective designating a living plant during two successive seasons.

Biological fight: Action of fighting crop pests using their natural enemies: pathogens, predators, or parasites, while reducing the use of chemical pesticides.

Biological nitrogen fixation: A process that produces protein substances from nitrogen gas in the atmosphere and the environment.

Brabant: Plough intended for flat ploughing

Breastfeeding: The operation of feeding young farm animals either with breast milk or with replacement milk.

Budburst: Budding, phase of recovery of vegetation and lengthening buds.

Bulb: An underground plant organ formed by a bud surrounded by fleshy leaves, allowing the plant to reform each year its aerial parts.

Bulbil: Bulging bud destined to detach itself from the plant that produced it and give birth to a new plant.

Calcicole: Adjective, which likes limestone soil.

Calcifuge: Adjective, which flees the limestone grounds.

Capital (capital goods): A set of resources used to produce goods and services. In economics, we now distinguish between physical capital (also called produced assets), natural capital, and human capital.

Catch culture: Culture set up on a plot between two main crops (example: clover)

Cereal: A cereal is a plant grown mainly for its seeds used in human nutrition and domestic animals

Chaptalization: The process of adding sugar to the must to increase the degree of final alcohol in the wine.

Charolais: French beef breed.

Cold hardening: Process of lignification of young branches of woody plants.

Collet: Transition zone between the root of a plant and its stem.

Colorado potato beetle: Insects of the order Coleoptera (*Leptinotarsa decemlineata*), with yellow elytra streaked with black, pests of potato leaves, and other Solanaceae.

Combine harvesters: Automatic agricultural machinery for harvesting seed crops, mainly cereals, in a single operation.

Comparative Advantage: A concept developed by the British economist David Ricardo, according to which economic agents — individuals, companies, countries — have the most efficiency when they stick to what they do best. This notion is of particular importance in world markets, where countries have the most to gain if they produce and export the goods and services they can produce in a more efficient way (at a lower cost, using less physical, human, and natural capital) than others. Ricardo has shown that a country can benefit from international trade even if it has higher production costs than its trading partners for all goods and services traded — in other words, even if it has no absolute advantage. To do this, it is a question of correctly choosing one's area of specialization at the international level according to its comparative advantages. In this case, the country will optimize its overall domestic production and consumption volume if it uses its export earnings to import other goods and services at prices that are lower than their domestic production costs.

Compost: Result of the aerobic decomposition of fresh organic matter (biomass) in a living and fertile product.

Cone: Reproductive organs of Gymnosperms.

Controlled designation of origin: Quality label for traditional French food products

Cover crops: Tandem disc gear sprayer for soil loosening

Crop rotation: First crop in a crop rotation.

Crop rotation: The distribution of the land of a farm in separate parts, called souls, each devoted to a given crop during a cropping season.

Cultivar (a contraction of cultivated variety): Is the result of selection (biology), hybridization or spontaneous mutation in plants.

Cultural rotation: Order of succession of crops on a given plot.

Current Assets: Portion of assets that is convertible into cash in the current year.

Debt: The sum of money that a physical or legal person must repay, usually with interest.

Demography: A scientific study of human populations, particularly in terms of numbers, composition, distribution, density, and growth, as well as the socioeconomic causes and consequences of the evolution of these factors.

Diversification: A strategy of choosing different investments. Some investments may involve a very high risk, other very low. By combining various investments in your portfolio, you can reduce the total risk level for a certain level of expected return.

Dividend: Part of the profit a company distributes to its shareholders in proportion to the shares they hold.

Drainage: The operation of artificially promoting the evacuation of excess water from the soil.

Economic development: Qualitative evolution and restructuring of a country's economy in relation to technological and social progress. The main indicator of economic development is the rise in gross national product (GNP) per capita (or GDP per capita), which reflects an increase in economic productivity and an improvement, on average, in the material well-being of the population of a country. Economic development and economic growth are closely linked.

Economic growth refers to the annual change in a country's wealth production: Growth is the engine of the market economy and is calculated by the evolution of the gross domestic product (GDP), measured in constant price to take into account the inflation. GDP is the sum of household consumption, business investment, state government expenditure, and net exports (exports minus imports) of a given country or territory.

Economic growth: Quantitative evolution or expansion of a country's economy. The commonly used indicator of economic growth is the percentage increase in gross domestic product (GDP) or gross national product (GNP) in a year. Economic growth takes two forms: an economy can grow "extensively" using resources (such as physical, human, or natural capital), or "intensive" using the same amount of resources more efficiently (so more productive). For economic growth is accomplished with more manpower, this does not result in increased per capita income. But when it comes to using and producing resources, including manpower, it is the result of the growth of the population. Intensive economic growth requires economic development.

Equity: The difference between the assets and liabilities of a company. This is what belongs to the owners of a company once the debts are deducted.

Essence: Synonymous with tree species among foresters.

Evapotranspiration: The amount of total water transferred from the soil to the atmosphere by evaporation at ground level and transpiration from plants.

Evergreen: This word refers to species, usually trees or shrubs that, like conifers, seem to never lose their leaves (or their "needles"); in fact, they lose their leaves in all seasons, but renew them also … in all seasons.

Exchange theory and econometrics: Models for determining exchange rates. Microstructure of the foreign exchange market. Models and methods for forecasting exchange rates. Trading platforms. Econometric methods for estimating exchange models.

Exchange traded fund: A fund whose securities are traded as shares on a stock exchange. These funds usually follow a benchmark. Unlike a mutual fund, the portfolio manager of the ETF is not mandated to maximize the return of the fund, but only to track the benchmark, which explains the generally lower management fees of the ETFs.

Externalities: Effects that the activities of one person or company have on others, without compensation. Externalities can harm or benefit others — in other words, be negative or positive. Example of negative externality: the situation created by a company which, to ensure its production, pollutes the local environment without providing compensation to the residents that it affects. In contrast, primary education can create positive externalities because it benefits not only primary school pupils but society as a whole. The state can limit negative externalities by regulating and taxing the products that create them. Conversely, it can reinforce positive externalities by subsidizing the products that carry them, or by directly supplying these products.

Farm: It is literally an agricultural exploitation operated under the system of renting and whose manager is the farmer.

Farming: An enterprise established for agricultural production and characterized by a unique management and own means of production.

Fertilization: The process of bringing to a growing medium, such as soil, the mineral elements necessary for the development of the plant.

Fertilizer: Mineral or organic substances intended to provide plants with nutrient supplements to enhance their growth and increase crop yield and quality.

Financial markets authorities: Organization that oversees Québec's financial markets and provides assistance to consumers of financial products and services. Its mission is to ensure the protection of the public by applying the laws and regulations on insurance, securities, deposit institutions (except banks), and the distribution of financial products and services.

Fire blight: Plant diseases of the Rosaceae family caused by the bacterium *Erwinia amylovora.*

Fish culture: Form of aquaculture consisting of fish farming.

Flow-Through Share: A share that may be issued by an oil, gas, or mining company. Since the holders participate in the exploration and development expenses, the flow-through shares may be eligible for deductions and tax credits that are usually only available to a corporation.

Fodder: Plants, or mixture of plants, cultivated for its vegetative parts (leaves, stems, possibly roots), that are used either in the fresh state, or preserved, generally by drying, for the feeding of animals.

Foreign direct investment: A foreign investment establishing a lasting interest in a company or allowing effective management control. It may consist of buying shares of a company based in another country, reinvesting the profits of a foreign-controlled enterprise in the country where it is based, or, in the case of parent companies, granting loans to their foreign subsidiaries. According to the rules of the International Monetary Fund, an investment constitutes a foreign direct investment if it is 10% of the shares of the foreign firm with voting rights, but many countries set a higher threshold because 10%, in many cases, it is not enough to establish effective control over the management of a company or, for an investor, to show a lasting interest in the company.

Foreign investment: Investment in a company that operates outside the investor's country. See also foreign direct investment and portfolio investment.

Fruit cultivation: Branches of arboriculture specialized in the cultivation of fruit trees to reap the fruits.

Fruit: Organs of the plant composed of seeds and their husks.

Fundamental Analysis: A method of evaluating the future value of a company or the value of its shares based on its financial health (financial statements), competitors, economic conditions, etc.

Futures contract: A contract that trades on a stock exchange and has standardized characteristics in terms of quantity, maturity, place of delivery, and quality of the good traded, which facilitates the transfer from one investor to another. Price is therefore the only element that fluctuates for the duration of the contract. A clearing house acts as an intermediary between the buyer and the seller and ensures that the contracts are respected: there is no counter-party risk.

GMO: A genetically modified organism, a living organism whose genetic heritage has been modified by genetic engineering.

GNP per capita: At the level of a country, the gross national product (GNP) divided by the number of inhabitants. Reflects the income that would be available to each individual if the GNP were evenly distributed. Also called per capita income. GNP per capita is a good indicator of economic productivity, but it does not reflect the level of well-being of the population or the degree of success of a country in development. It does not show the extent to which a country's income is evenly or equitably distributed among its inhabitants, does not reflect the damage to the environment and natural resources caused by production processes, and does not take into account the unpaid work that can be done within households or communities, or the production to be put to the account of the black economy (occult). It attributes value to everything that is produced, whether the element in question undermines or contributes to the general well-being (for example, chemical weapons, and medicines), but it ignores the value of elements of the property — being individual such as leisure or freedom.

Grassland: Term referring to natural or artificial grasslands.

Green Fertilizer: A temporary crop that is intended to be buried quickly to provide nutrients to the next crop.

Gross domestic investment rates: All expenditures to replace and increase a country's physical capital, plus changes in the level of product inventories, as a percentage of GDP. Gross domestic investment, along with foreign direct investment, is essential for economic growth and economic development.

Gross domestic product: Value of all goods and services produced in a country in a year (see also Gross National Product). GDP can be calculated by adding up all the elements of income: wages, interests, profits, rents or, on the contrary, of expenditure: consumption, investment, public purchases, net exports (exports minus imports), of an economy. In either case, the result should be the same because an expense is always matched by income, so the sum of all earnings must be equal to the sum of all expenses.

Gross domestic savings rate: Rate equal to gross domestic product (GDP) minus public and private sector consumption, expressed as a percentage of GDP. A high rate is usually indicative of a high investment potential for a country. See also savings.

Gross national product: The value of all goods and services produced in a country in a year (gross domestic product), plus income received from abroad by residents of the country, minus those paid to nonresidents. It can be well below the GDP if a country's production income is largely derived from foreign individuals or firms. Conversely, if nationals or companies of a country hold a large volume of shares and bonds of companies or public bodies of other countries from which they receive income, GNP may be greater than GDP. But for most countries, these two statistical indicators present negligible differences. The term "gross" indicates that the impairment loss related to the natural "depreciation" of capital used for production is not deducted from the value of total output. If it were, we would get an indicator called net domestic product, also called national income. The terms "product" and "income" are often used interchangeably, so the term income per capita is also used to refer to GNP per capita.

Growth, technical progress, and employment: Technical progress covers all the knowledge that enables productivity gains or the emergence of new products. It is based on research and results in innovations (products, processes, opportunities, raw materials, or organization, according to the five types listed by Joseph Schumpeter). Productivity gains are an essential source of growth, but can have negative effects on employment when they are larger than the growth itself.

Harrow: Agricultural instrument consisting of a grid-shaped frame with short teeth allowing a superficial working of the soil.

Harvest: Harvesting cereals.

Hedge Fund: Funds issued in the form of units. The manager of this fund has great flexibility in the investment strategies that can be used. These strategies are often referred to as "alternative investment strategies." This fund is usually managed so that its return is not influenced by changes in the stock and bond markets. As a general rule, it consists of investments that may only be suitable for experienced investors: private equity, derivatives, futures, etc. The same is true of the strategies used, including short selling, debt investment, concentration of investments, and investment in companies in financial difficulty.

Hedge: Association of shrubs or trees generally planted and maintained to form a fence or protection against the wind.

Herbicide: Active substance or preparation with the property of killing plants.

Hilling: Operations intended to bring back the ground to the foot of the plants, in the form of buttes.

Hoeing: In agriculture and gardening, hoeing is loosening the surface layer of soil around cultivated plants.

Humification: Process of transformation of organic matter into humus under the influence of the microfauna and the microflora of the soil.

Humus: Blackish residue resulting from the decomposition in the soil of organic waste under the action of detritivore organisms (bacteria, fungi, and arthropods), likely to take the colloidal state.

Insecticide: Active substance or preparation with the property of killing insects.

Insured capital: Amount of money provided for in an insurance contract that is paid to the beneficiary of the insurance if the risk covered is realized.

Investment: Expenditures made by individuals, businesses, or public entities to increase their capital. From the point of view of individual economic agents, the acquisition of property rights for an existing capital is also an investment. But from the point of view of an economy as a whole, only the creation of new capital is considered an investment. Investment is a necessary condition for economic growth. See savings, gross domestic savings rate, and gross domestic investment rates.

Investment: In economics, investment refers to the flow that feeds the capital stock. At the technical level, National Accounts refer to investment as "gross fixed capital formation" (GFCF), "value of durable goods acquired by production units to be used for at least one year in their production process." Investment is one of the "engines" of growth, in particular because it is the main vector of technological progress.

Irrigation: Operations of artificially bringing water to cultivated plants to increase production and allow their normal development in case of water deficit.

Issuer: A person who issues or proposes to issue a security in exchange for capital raised from investors. This person is usually a legal person, for example a corporation or a mutual fund. An issuer solicits money from investors to improve its financial position, to carry out projects or to develop new markets. In compensation for the money invested, the investor receives a security that may be, among other things, a listed stock or an obligation.

Languages: English and computer language. English specific to bank, stock markets, and exchange rates. Vocabulary acquisition and learning to read graphs and financial charts.

Lateral roots: Very small secondary roots.

Leverage effect: Borrowing money for the purpose of investing amplifies the potential gains, as well as the potential losses, of any investment. Debt investing therefore increases risk and should be viewed with caution by investors. If you are thinking of borrowing money for the purpose of investing, be sure to evaluate the value of the loss that may be incurred if the value of your investment falls.

Liming: Adding calcium or calcium magnesium additives to a soil to correct acidity.

Livestock: All agricultural operations intended to ensure the reproduction of animals and their maintenance for use (work, leisure) or their products (meat, milk, leather, etc.).

Livestock: Collective term for gray livestock. There are cattle (cattle, horses, mules, donkeys) and small livestock (sheep, goats, pigs).

Long-term debt (noncurrent debt): The sum of money that a natural or legal person must repay, usually with interest. However, the sum is not due for a year.

Marcescent: Adjective is said of a plant whose dead leaves persist all winter.

Margins buying: Borrow money to invest. This amplifies the potential gains, as well as the potential losses of any investment (leverage). Margins buying therefore increases risk and should be viewed with caution by investors. Also called debt investment.

Market Capitalization: The valuation of a company's value obtained by multiplying the number of common shares of the company by its market value.

Market failures: Situations in which a market economy does not provide the population with the desired quantity of certain goods and services. They can intervene when the market does not produce enough public goods and goods with positive externalities, when it produces too much good with negative externalities, when the game of natural monopolies has the effect of inflating the prices of the products, and when the economic agents do not have access to sufficient information, such as those relating to the quality of certain consumer goods. These shortcomings generally justify the economic intervention of the state, but there is always a risk of state failure — the kind of situation in which deficiencies in strategy processes or institutional structures prevent government measures to effectively improve social welfare.

Market liberalization: The process of eliminating or no longer employing state control measures that impede the normal functioning of a market economy — for example, the elimination of price and wage controls and quotas import, or reduce taxes and tariffs. In general, liberalization of the market does not mean that the state completely refrains from intervening in market processes.

Milking machine: Machine for milking cattle.

Mineralization: Decomposition of the organic part of a material that also contains a mineral part. For example: composting, burning.

Monoculture: A particular form of crop rotation in which a single crop is maintained in a given plot for several years.

Mussel farming: Form of aquaculture consisting of mussel farming.

Mutual aid (agriculture): System of equalization of labor in agriculture.

Natural phosphate: Fertilizer consisting of soft ground phosphates.

Net private capital flows: Private sector capital flows received by a country at market conditions, minus similar outflows. Net portfolio investment flows are an example: they are all stocks and bonds acquired by foreign investors, less the value of the shares and shares they sold. See portfolio investment.

Net public aid: All grants and concessional loans granted by donor country governments to recipient countries minus any principal repayments made during the term of the loans in question.

Nitrate: Ion NO_3^- which is the form of nitrogen assimilated by plants.

Nitrates: Salts of nitric acid, many of which are used as fertilizers.

Nitrification: A process that takes place in the soil under the action of specific microorganisms that leads to the conversion of ammonia to assimilable nitrate by plants.

Nitrogen cycle: A biogeochemical cycle that describes the succession of modifications undergone by the different forms of nitrogen (nitrogen, nitrate, nitrite, ammonia, organic nitrogen (proteins)).

Nonprofit organization that protects policyholders in the event of insolvency of their life insurance company: Funded by industry, it administers the industry's consumer guarantee fund.

Oilseeds: A plant grown specifically for its high-fat seeds or fruits, from which oil for food, energy, or industrial use is extracted.

Ordinary Share: Share of property issued by a corporation. As the owner, the holder of common shares generally has the right to elect directors and vote on certain decisions regarding the activities of the corporation. He is usually entitled to a share of the remaining assets of the corporation if it is dissolved. Ordinary shares give the right to receive dividends, if such dividends are declared by the company. This type of share does not have a deadline.

Organic agriculture: A mode of agricultural production that does not use synthetic chemicals or limits their use.

Oyster farming: Form of aquaculture consisting of oyster farming.

Permaculture: A mode of production aimed at creating a sustainable agricultural system, saving energy (manual and mechanical work, fuel, etc.) and respectful of living beings and their mutual relations.

Persistent: Refers to an organ, including leaves, which remain in place each season.

Phylloxera: Homopterous insects (*Dactylosphaera vitifoliae*), which is a kind of pest aphid of the vine.

Phytosanitary products: A product intended to protect cultivated plant species and to improve their yields, consisting of an active substance or a combination of several chemical substances or microorganisms, a binder and optionally accompanied by a solvent, adjuvants, or surfactant.

Plough: A ploughing tool used to plough the fields and turning the soil sideways.

Pollination: Transport of pollen from the anther to the stigma of the same or another flower.

Portfolio investment: Purchase of stocks and bonds, which, unlike a direct investment, do not establish a lasting interest in a company nor does it make it possible to control its management effectively. See foreign direct investment.

Poultry farming: Breeding of poultry and more generally birds.

Privileged share with cumulative dividends: A share that includes a privilege whereby dividends that are not paid on a scheduled date must all be paid before a dividend can be offered to the common shareholders.

Privileged share: A share that is issued by a company. The investor who buys it therefore owns a share of property in this company. A preferred share usually gives the holder the right to receive a fixed dividend before dividends are paid to the common shareholders of the corporation.

Production factors: Main means used for any production. Economists used to distinguish three factors of production: labor, land, and capital. More recently, they have come to appeal to the three notions of capital: physical capital (or product), human capital, and natural capital.

Productivity (economic productivity, output): Production of goods and services expressed on a unit basis in relation to the means used: for example, per unit of labor (labor productivity), energy (as for the measurement of GNP per unit of energy used), or of all the factors of combined production.

Public goods: Goods with the dual characteristic of nonrivalry (the consumption that one makes of it does not reduce their availability for others) and nonexclusion (one cannot prevent those who want to consume them). As a result, it is impossible to make their consumption pay, which is why the private sector is not interested in the supply of these goods, which is in fact provided in many cases by the State. Public goods are usually national or local. Defense is a national public good that benefits the people of a whole country. Rural roads are local public goods that benefit a smaller group of people. There may also be global public goods, which benefit the majority of the world's population: for example, peace and global security, or the information needed to prevent global climate change. The provision of goods (and services) of this type is a function of international organizations.

Rational agriculture: Agricultural production method designed to optimize the economic result by controlling the quantities of inputs, and in particular the chemical substances used (pesticides, fertilizers) in order to limit their impact on the environment.

Redeemable share at the option of the company: A share that the issuing corporation may redeem at any time at a specified price. The corporation may, however, have conditions to fulfil in order to exercise its privilege. For example, the shares could only be redeemable after a given period, for example 5 years.

Redeemable share at the option of the holder: A share for which the owner has the right to request a refund on a predetermined date and condition.

Registered shareholder: A shareholder whose name is registered in the books or records of a corporation on a particular day. The fact that a shareholder is registered or not is important, especially in the case of dividend distribution. For example, if a corporation declares a dividend for registered shareholders, only the shareholders who are listed in the books on the given date will receive the expected dividends.

Rhizome: Perennial underground stem, very often horizontal, emitting each year roots and aerial stems.

Risk and financial engineering: General typology of financial instruments and derivatives in the main asset markets: theoretical aspects of price formation in these markets. OTC (swaps, caps, and floors) and second-generation instruments (look back option, Asian options). Quantitative methods for measuring risk exposure in banks. Derivatives and structure on currencies and equities, hedging and rate structure, credit derivatives.

Risk management: Risk management is the discipline that seeks to identify and methodologically treat risks related to the activities of an organization, regardless of the nature or origin of these risks. As such, it is a component of the strategy that aims to reduce the likelihood of failure or uncertainty of all factors that may affect the organism. Beyond the financial risk management and the cleavage between financial and nonfinancial risks, the risk analysis of the company imposes an extended watch that can be likened to economic intelligence. This prevention of the risks weighing on the assets results in establishing a grid of the risks with each time-targeted watch adapted to each type of risks (strategy, legal, social, environmental, etc.). The phenomenon of cause and effect is more and more difficult to analyze with the systemic effect that financial globalization and the open or globalized economy can now have.

Root: Not visible part of the plant drawing from the ground the elements necessary for its nutrition (water, mineral salts).

Roots nodules: Small blisters forming on the roots of certain species of plants, in particular the Fabaceae, under the action of bacteria of the genus Rhizobium living in symbiosis with the plant.

Rootstock: In arboriculture, a subject on which a graft is implanted.

Savings: Revenues not allocated to current consumption. See also gross domestic savings rate and gross domestic investment rates.

Seed: Fertilized eggs which, after dispersion and germination, gives new plants.

Segregated funds: Funds issued by insurers. It is a fund similar to a mutual fund, but with additional guarantees. For example, in case of death, you could be assured of recovering the amounts invested even if the value of your investments dropped. You could also benefit from a guarantee at term. The invested assets are held by an insurer separately from its other assets, hence the term "segregated funds."

Services: Intangible goods whose production and consumption often occur simultaneously. To take an example in the field of education, the course which students attend — and which constitutes a teaching service — is taught simultaneously by the teacher. The service sector includes hotels, restaurants, and wholesale and retail; transportation, storage and communications; finance, insurance, real estate, and business services; community and social services (such as education and healthcare); and personal services.

Share capital: Part of the equity of a joint-stock company that represents the contributions of the shareholders.

Share division: The process of allocating two or more shares for each outstanding share. For example, a 2 for 1 division would double the number of shares outstanding. However, the value of each share would decrease by half, so that the shareholders' financial situation does not change as a result of this transaction.

Share: Property document issued by a company. The shares are issued by the companies and they represent a part of ownership.

Shareholder: It is the natural or legal person who holds common or preferred shares of one or more companies.

Soil: Natural surface formation, with loose structure and variable thickness, resulting from the transformation of the underlying bedrock under the influence of various processes, physical, chemical, and biological, in contact with the atmosphere and beings alive (Albert Demolon).

Sources and limits of growth: Economic growth is the increase in wealth produced by men. If it results in a rise in the standard of living and an improvement in the way of life, it brings in its wake negative externalities, which cast doubt on the reliability of its measurement.

Spike: Inflorescence with flowers arranged around a central axis, without a pedicel or with a very short pedicel.

Spikelet: A secondary spike that, when grouped with others, forms an ear or panicle.

Stable: Livestock building for housing equines (horses, donkeys, etc.)

Stanchion: Metal part supporting working parts in a plough.

Stock exchange: An organized market where securities are traded, such as equities or derivatives.

Stock market share: Share of a company traded on the stock exchange. For a company to be registered, it must meet certain criteria, rules and regulations, and pay admission fees.

Stubble cultivation: A cultivation method consisting of a superficial soil work intended to bury stubble and remains of straw to promote their decomposition.

Stud: Establishment in which the breeding stock of the equine species is maintained for the multiplication and improvement of the breeds.

Sty: Livestock building intended to house pigs.

Subordinate share: Share that has limited voting rights or no voting rights, unless special circumstances exist.

Subsidiary: Company controlled by a parent company. The parent company may derive economic benefits from the controlled corporation and assume the associated risks.

Subsoiling: Technique to restore soil permeability.

Swath: Fodder strip left on the field after mowing.

Swivel: Is said to be a very large root in relation to rootlets and sinking vertically into the soil (example: carrot).

Systemic insecticide: An insecticide that penetrates the plant tissue and is carried by the sap.

Tax base: The amount to which the tax or taxation rate applies. It corresponds to the taxable income.

Technical analysis: A method of evaluating the future value of a company's stock, based in particular on the analysis of charts illustrating the share price and the volume of transactions.

Terms of exchange. Relationship between export prices and import prices: A high ratio is advantageous for an economy, since the country concerned can then finance a large volume of imports through a limited volume of exports. In the event of a deterioration of the terms of trade, the country will have to export more to obtain the same volume of imports.

The economic situation is the state of the market during a specific period (one quarter, one year): The term is used to characterize the different phases of economic cycles. And these different phases do not benefit (or harm) everyone in the same way.

The financial market ensures the circulation of funds necessary for the functioning of the economy, includes the capital market, for investment or other long-term employment; the money market, for short-term credit and advance operations. Although the financial market is often identified with the stock market, it is important to know that investment banks and other credit institutions play an increasingly important role in the collection and distribution of long-term capital.

The stock market, where shares and bonds are traded: Has long been considered as an ingenious and ideal system for collecting individual savings, even modest ones, and to direct them towards important companies, likely to make with this money productive investments, and thus to foster economic development. In addition, the stock market was considered an almost perfect model of free competition according to the criteria of the liberal economy.

The water cycle: The hydrological cycle is a model representing flows between large reservoirs of liquid, solid, or gaseous water, on Earth.

Theory and econometrics of banking and insurance: Banking institutions and regulatory foundations. Interest rate and credit risk models. Economic models of insurance. Multivariate models, copula functions, variable conditional correlation models. Parametric and nonparametric methods of efficiency boundaries. Models of the production curve and empirical applications.

Theory and econometrics of derivative product information extraction: Asset price models and extraction methods, from option prices, price distribution density. Initiation to use MATLAB software to evaluate derivatives.

Theory and econometrics of financial markets: Theoretical foundations of market finance and specific problems of portfolio management. Aspects of empirical finance and forecasting. Introduction to conditional heteroscedasticity models and nonlinear dynamic models. Modeling financial series.

Tillage tool: A tool or a machine used to tillage, that is to say to loosen it, plough it, and hoe it.

Tiller: Motorized agricultural machine for the work of the earth, generally of weak power, and whose conduct is ensured by a man on foot.

Transfer payments: Amounts paid by the state to individuals as a redistribution of a country's wealth. These include, for example, payments for pensions, social benefits, and unemployment benefits.

Treasury bill: Title issued by the federal and provincial governments. This is a loan made by the investor to the issuing government. It is sold in large denominations, starting at $1000 and the term is at most one year.

Underlying asset: Assets from which the value of a derivative is determined. (option to buy or sell, futures, etc.)

Vegetative multiplication: Asexual reproduction method used in plants.

Woody: Refers to a plant whose stem has the consistency of wood, thanks to the lignin it contains.

REFERENCES

ABB Bomem inc. (2001). *MR Series Spectroradiometers User Manual.* Québec: ABB Bomem.

Acemoglu, D (2009). *Introduction to Economic Growth.* Princeton: Princeton University Press.

Acemoglu, D (2009). *Introduction to Modern Economic Growth.* Princeton: Princeton University Press.

Acemoglu, D, P Aghion P and F Zilibotti (2003). Vertical integration and distance to frontier. *Journal of European Economic Association*, 630–638.

Acemoglu, D, P Aghion and F Zilibotti (March 2006a). Distance to frontier, selection, and economic growth, *Journal of the European Economic Association*, 4(1), 37–74.

Adams, ML, WA Norvell, WD Philpot and JH Peverly (2000). Spectral detection of micronutrient deficiency in 'Bragg' soybean. *Agronomy Journal*, 92, 261–268.

Adeyemi, SB and TO Fagbemi (2010). Audit quality, corporate governance and firm characteristics in Nigeria. *International Journal of Business and Management*, 5(5), 169–179.

Admanti, AR and P Pfleiderer (1988). A theory of intraday trading patterns: Volume and price variability. *Review of Financial Studies*, 1, 3–40.

Agence Canadienne d'inspection des aliments (2001). Variété de pommes de terre. 2002.

Aghion, P *et al.* (2005). *Volatility and Growth: Financial Development and the Cyclical Behavior of the Composition of Investment.* Mimeo: Harvard University.

Aghion, P and P. Howitt (1998). *Endogenous Growth Theory*, p. 694. Cambridge: MIT Press.

Aghion, P and P Howitt (2010). *L'Economie de la Croissance*, Paris: Economica.

Aghion P, P Howitt and D Mayer-Foulkes (February 2005). The effect of financial development on convergence: Theory and evidence. *Quarterly Journal of Economics*, 120, 173–222.

Aghion P and G Saint-Paul (1998). Uncovering some causal relationships between productivity growth and the structure of economic fluctuations: A tentative survey. *Labor*, 12, 279–303.

Agriculture and Agroalimentaire Canada (2000a). *Indicateurs agro-environnementaux*. 2002.

Agriculture and Agroalimentaire Canada (2000b). *L'agriculture écologiquement durable au Canada: Rapport sur le projet des indicateurs agroenvironnementaux*. McRae, T, CAS Smith and LJ Gregorich (éd). Ottawa (Ontario).

Agriculture and Agroalimentaire Canada (2001). *L'agriculture en harmonie avec la nature II*—Stratégie de développement durable d'Agriculture et Agroalimentaire Canada 2001–2004, 77.

Agvise Laboratories (2002). *Plant Nutrient Analysis Sampling Guide*. Northwood: Agvise Laboratories.

Ahmet, F (2006). The Effects of Volatility on Growth and Financial Development through Capital Market Imperfections, MPRA, Working Paper No 5486.

Alard, V (2002). *A la recherche d'une agriculture durable: Étude de systèmes herbagers économes en Bretagne*, p. 340. Paris: INRA.

Allard, G (2000). *L'agriculture biologique face à son développement: les enjeux futurs*, p. 394. Paris: INRA.

Alonso-Bonis, S and P de Andrés-Alonso (2007). Ownership structure and performance in large Spanish companies. Empirical evidence in the context of an endogenous relation. *Corporate Ownership & Control*, 4(4), 206–216.

Amihud, Y and H Mendelson (1987). Trading mechanisms and stock returns: An empirical investigation. *The Journal of Finance*, 42, 533–553.

Analytical Spectral Device Inc. (2000). *FieldSpec Pro® User Guide*. Boulder: ASD Inc.

Andjelkovic, A, G Boyle and W McNoe (2002). Public disclosure of executive compensation: Do shareholders need to know? *Pacific-Basin Finance Journal*, 10(1), 97–117.

André, JC *et al.* (1988). Evaporation over land surfaces: First results from HAPEX-MOBILHY special observing period. *Annales Geophysical*, 6, 477–492.

Antoniou, A, P Holmes and R Priestley (1998). The effects of stock index futures trading on stock index volatility: An analysis of the asymmetric response of volatility to news. *Journal of Futures Markets*, 18, 151–166.

Arestis, P and P Demetriades (1996). Finance and Growth: Institutional Considerations and Causality, Working Paper 9605, University of East London, Department of Economics.

Arestis, P and P Demetriades (1998). Finance and growth: Is Schumpeter right? *Analyse Economica*, 16 (30), 5–21.

Argouarch, J, V Lecomte and JM Morin (2008). *Maraîchage Biologique.* 2ème éd. pp. 265. Dijon: Educagri.

Assemblée Nationale du Québec (2001). Projet de loi no 184 — Loi modifiant la Loi sur la protection du territoire et des activités agricole et d'autres dispositions législatives. Code civil du Québec. Québec: Éditeur officiel du Québec: 19.

Atherton, BC *et al.* (1999). Site-specific farming: A perspective on information needs, benefits and limitations. *Journal of Soil and Water Conservation*, 54(2), 455–461.

Aubert, C and G Fléchet (2007). *Quelle agriculture pour quelle alimentation*, p. 118. Toulouse: Terre sauvage.

Auernhammer, H (2001). Precision farming-the environmental challenge. *Computers and Electronics in Agriculture*, 30, 31–43.

Bai, CE *et al.* (2004). Corporate governance and market valuation in China. *Journal of Comparative Economics*, 32(4), 599–616.

Banghøj, J *et al.* (2010). Determinants of executive compensation in privately held firms. *Accounting & Finance*, 50(3), 481–510.

Bariou, R, D Lecamus and FL Henaff (1985). *Indices de végétation, Rennes: Centre régional de Télédétection*, p. 2. Rennes: Presses Universitaires de Rennes.

Barneto, P (1998). Mécanismes d'échange et comportement des cours des contrats à terme: Une étude empirique sur les principaux marchés régionaux. *Banque & Marchés* 35, 9–16.

Barro, R and X Sala-i-Martin (1995). *Economic Growth*, p. 539. New York: McGraw Hill.

Baysinger, BD and HN Butler (1985). Corporate governance and the board of directors: Performance effects of changes in board composition. *Journal of Law, Economics & Organization*, 1(1), 101–124.

Beau, C (2005). *En Méditerranée... les jardiniers de l'avenir*, p. 141. La Motte d'Aigues: les 3 spirales.

Beaulieu, D *et al.* (1990). *Guide de la Géomatique.* Sainte-Foy: Ordre des arpenteurs-géomètres du Québec.

Beck, T and A Demirg c-Kunt (2009). Financial Institutions and Markets across Countries and over Time: Data and Analysis, World Bank Policy Research, Working Paper No. 4943, May 2009.

Beck, T, A Demirg¨c-Kunt and R Levine (2001). The financial structure database. In *Financial Structure and Economic Growth: A Cross-Country Comparison of Banks, Markets, and Development*, A Demirguc-Kunt and R Levine (eds.), pp. 17–80. Cambridge: MIT Press.

Beck, T and R Levine (2002). Industry growth and capital allocation: Does having a market- or bank-based system matter? *Journal of Financial Economics*, 64, 147–180.

Beck, T and R Levine (2004). Stock markets, banks and growth: Panel evidence. *Journal of Banking and Finance*, 28, 423–442.

Becker, B *et al.* (1992). Automated securities trading. *Journal of Financial Research*, 4, 327–341.

Becker, K, J Finnerty and K Kopecky (1996). Macroeconomic news and the efficiency of international bond futures markets. *Journal of Futures Markets*, 16, 131–145.

Bencivenga, VR and BD Smith (1991). Financial intermediation and endogenous growth. *Review of Economics Studies*, 58, 195–209.

Bencivenga, VR and BD Smith (1993). Some consequences of credit rationing in an endogenous growth model. *Journal of Economic Dynamics and Control*, 17, 97–122.

Berkman, H and L Hayes (2000). The role of floor brokers in the supply of liquidity: An empirical analysis. *Journal of Futures Markets*, 20, 205–218.

Bernard, JL, P Havet and M Fort (2007). *Productions Végétales, Pratiques Agricoles et Faune Sauvage: Pour une Agriculture Performante et Durable.* p. 251. Boulogne: Union des industries de la protection des plantes.

Bertrand, J (2001). *Agriculture et Biodiversité: Un Partenariat à Valoriser.* Dijon: Educagri.

Bessembinder, H and P Seguin (1993). Price volatility, trading volume and market depth: Evidence from futures markets. *Journal of Financial and Quantitative Analysis*, 28, 21–40.

Beukema, HP and DEVD Zaag (1990). *Introduction to Potato Production.* Wageningen: PUDOC.

Bhattacharya, M (1983). Transactions data tests of efficiency of the Chicago board options exchange. *Journal of Financial Economics*, 12, 161–185.

Bhattacharya, M (1986). Direct Tests of Bid-Ask Spreads Models, Working Paper, University of Michigan.

Biais, B, T Foucault and P Hillion (1997). *Microstructure des marchés financiers. Institutions, modèles et tests empiriques.* Paris: PUF.

Blackmer, TM *et al.* (1996). Nitrogen deficiency detection using reflected shortwave radiation from irrigated corn canopies. *Agronomy Journal,* 88(1), 1–5.

Blackmer, TM, JS Schepers and GE Varvel (1994). Light reflectance compared with other nitrogen stress measurements in corn leaves. *Agronomy Journal,* 86, 934–938.

Blackmer, TM, JS Schepers and MF Vigil (1993). Chlorophyll meter readings in corn as affected by plant spacing. *Communications in Soil Science and Plant analysis,* 24(17/18), 2507–2516.

Blanchard, O and S Fischer (1989). *Lectures on Macroeconomics,* p. 650. Cambridge: MIT Press.

Booth, G, R So and Y Tse (1999). Price discovery in the German equity index derivatives markets. *Journal of Futures Markets,* 19, 619–643.

Breedon, FJ and A Holland (1998). *Electronic Versus Open Outcry Markets: The Case of the Bund Futures Contract,* Document 76. Bank of England.

Brorsen, BW (1989). Liquidity costs and scalping returns in the corn futures markets. *Journal of Futures Markets,* 9, 225–236.

Brown, LD and Caylor, ML (2004). *Corporate Governance Study: The Correlation between Corporate Governance and Company Performance.* Corporate Governance Study, Institutional Shareholder Services.

Buschmann, C and E Nagel (1993). In vivo spectroscopy and internal optics of leaves as basis for remote sensing of vegetation. *International Journal of Remote Sensing,* 14, 711–722.

Cambouris, A (2000). Agriculture de précision et agriculture durable: deux approches à intégrer. In *Ier colloque sur la géomatique agricole et l'agriculture de précision,* St-Hyacinthe, Quebec23 et 24 mars 2000.

Cameron, AC and PK Trivedi (2009). *Microeconometrics using Stata,* Vol. 5. College Station: Stata Press.

Carter, GA and AK Knapp (2001). Leaf optical properties in higher plants: Linking spectral characteristics to stress and chlorophyll concentration. *American Journal of Botany,* 88(4), 677–684.

Carter, GA and BA Spiering (2002). Optical properties of intact leaves for estimating chlorophyll concentration. *Journal of Environmental Quality,* 31, 1424–1432.

Carter, GA, WG Cibula and RL Miller (1996). Narrow-band reflectance imagery compared with thermal imagery for early detection of plant stress. *Journal of Plant Physiology,* 148, 515–522.

Carter, GA and RL Miller (1994). Early detection of plant stress by digital imaging within narrow stress-sensitive waveband. *Remote Sensing of Environment*, 50, 295–302.

Centre Canadien de Télédétection (2002). Glossaire de télédétection du CCT, Ressources Naturelles Canada. 2003.

Chaerle, L *et al.* (1999). Presymptomatic visualization of plant-virus interactions by thermography. *Nature Biotechnology*, 17, 813–816.

Chaerle, L *et al.* (1–4 April 2002). Visualisation of early stress response in plant leaves, Thermosense XXIV, Proceedings of SPIE, Orlando.

Chaerle, L and DVD Straten (2000). Imaging techniques and the early detection of plant stress. *Trends in Plant Science*, 5(11), 495–501.

Chakraborty, S and R Ray (2004). *Bank-Based versus Market-Based Financial Systems: A Growth-Theoretic Analysis.* Mimeo: University of Oregon (Department of Economics).

Charles, N and P Charles (1982). Trends and random walk in macroeconomic time series: Some evidence and implications, *Journal of Monetary Economics*, 10(2), 139–162.

Cheng, S, JH Evans Iii and NJ Nagarajan (2008). Board size and firm performance: The moderating effects of the market for corporate control. *Review of Quantitative Finance and Accounting*, 31(2), 121–145.

Cheung, Y and L Ng (1990). The dynamics of S&P 500 index and S&P 500 futures intraday price volatilities. *Review of Futures Markets*, 9, 458–486.

Cho, MH (1998). Ownership structure, investment, and the corporate value: An empirical analysis. *Journal of Financial Economics*, 47(1), 103–121.

Choi, H and A Subrahmanyam (1994). Using intraday data to test for effects of index futures on the underlying stock markets. *Journal of Futures Markets*, 14, 293–322.

Clyman, D, C Allen and R Jaycobs (1997). Liquidity without volume: The case of FINEX, Dublin. *Journal of Futures Markets*, 17, 247–277.

Clyman, D and R Jaycobs (1998). Liquidity without volume. II. Using block orders to measure market resiliency. *Journal of Futures Markets*, 18, 281–296.

Commissaire à l'environnement et au développement durable (2001). *Rapport de la commissaire à l'environnement et au développement durable à la Chambre des Communes.* Ottawa: Bureau du vérificateur général du Canada.

Cornell, B (2000). The relationship between volume and price variability in futures markets, *Journal of Futures Markets*, 20, 5–18.

Costa, C *et al.* (2001). Inter-relationships of applied nitrogen, SPAD, and yields of leafy and non-leafy maize genotypes. *Journal of Plant Nutrition*, 24(8), 1173–1194.

CPVQ (1996). *Grilles de référence en fertilisation*, 2nd Ed. CPVQ (Conseil des productions végétales du Québec).

CPVQ (2000). *Guide des pratiques de conservation en grandes cultures.*

CRAAQ (2003). *La géomatique appliquée à l'agriculture de précision.* Publication Vu 067.

Crain, S and J Lee (1995). Intraday volatility in interest rate and foreign exchange spot and futures markets. *Journal of Futures Markets*, 15, 395–421.

Crespo, S (2007). *L'inégalité de revenu au Québec 1979–2004: les contributions de composantes de revenu selon le cycle économique.* Québec: Institut de la statistique du Québec.

Cutter, EG (1992). Structure and development of the potato plant. In *The Potato Crop*, P Harris (ed.) Vol. 1, p. 909. London: Chapman & Hall.

Daigler, R (1997). Intraday futures volatility and theories of market behavior. *Journal of Futures Markets*, 17, 45–74.

Dalton, DR *et al.* (1999). Number of directors and financial performance: A meta-analysis. *Academy of Management Journal*, 42(6), 674–686.

Demirg-Kunt Asli, E Feyen and R Levine (2011). Optimal Financial Structures and Development: The evolving importance of banks and markets, World Bank Policy Research Working Paper, N 5805, June 3, 2011.°

Demirg-Kunt, A and R Levine (2001a). Financial structure and economic growth: Perspectives and lessons. In *Financial Structure and Economic Growth: A Cross-Country Comparison of Banks, Markets, and Development*, A Demirg-Kunt and R Levine (eds.), pp. 3–14. Cambridge: MIT Press.

Demirg-Kunt, A and R Levine (2001b). Bank-based and market-based financial systems: Cross-country comparisons. In *Financial Structure and Economic Growth: A Cross-Country Comparison of Banks, Markets, and Development*, A Demirguc-Kunt and R Levine (eds.), pp. 81–140. Cambridge: MIT Press.

Demsetz, H and B Villalonga (2001). Ownership structure and corporate performance. *Journal of Corporate Finance*, 7(3), 209–233.

Ding, DK (1999). The determinants of bid-ask spreads in the foreign exchange futures market: A microstructure analysis. *Journal of Futures Markets*, 19, 307–324.

Docking, D, I Kawaller and P Koch (1999). Mid-day volatility spikes in U.S. futures markets. *Journal of Futures Markets*, 19, 195–216.

Domowitz, I (1990). The mechanics of automated trade execution systems. *Journal of Financial Intermediation,* 1, 167–194.

Dosi, G *et al.* (1988). *Technical Change and Economic Theory.* London and New York: Pinter Publishers.

Dubreuille, S (2000). *Liquidité et formation des prix sur le Matif.* Paris: Economica.

Dwyer, LM *et al.* (1994). Quantifying the nonlinearity in chlorophyll meter response to corn leaf nitrogen concentration. *Canadian Journal of Plant Science,* 75(1), 179–182.

Dwyer, LM, M Tollepaar and L Houwing (1991). A nondestructive method to monitor leaf greenness in corn. *Canadian Journal of Plant Science,* 71, 505–509.

Eckman, PD (1992). Intraday patterns in the S&P 500 index futures market. *Journal of Futures Markets,* 12, 365–372.

Edwards, F (1988). Futures trading and cash market volatility: Stock index and interest rate futures. *Journal of Futures Markets,* 8, 421–439.

Eltony, MN and M Babiker (2005). Arab capital markets development and institutions. *Journal of Economic and Administrative Sciences,* 21(1), 42–63.

Ergungor, OE (2004). Market vs. bank-based financial systems: Do rights and regulations really matter? *Journal of Banking and Finance,* 28, 2869–2887.

Fama, E and M Jensen (1983). Separation of ownership and control. *Journal of Law and Economics,* 26(2), 301–325.

Farooque, O *et al.* (2010). Co-deterministic relationship between ownership concentration and corporate performance: Evidence from an emerging economy. *Accounting Research Journal,* 23(2), 172–189.

Farquhar, GD *et al.* (1989). Photosynthesis and gaz exchange. In *Plants under Stress,* HG Jones, TJ Flowers and MB Jones (eds.), pp. 47–69. New York: Cambridge University Press.

Fatas, A (2002). The Effects of Business Cycles on Growth, Central Bank of Chile, Working Paper, No 156, Central Bank of Chile.

Fauzi, F and S Locke (2012). Board structure, ownership structure and firm performance: A study of New Zealand listed-firms. *Asian Academy of Management Journal of Accounting and Finance,* 8(2), 43–67.

Feinstone, L (1987). Minute by minute: Efficiency, normality and randomness in intradaily asset prices. *Journal of Applied Econometrics,* 2, 193–214.

Ferguson, A, JR Francis, and DJ Stokes (2003). The effects of firm-wide and office-level industry expertise on audit pricing. *The Accounting Review,* 78(2), 429–448.

Filbeck, G, and SK Lee (2006). Board size and firm performance: The case of small firms. *Academy of Accounting and Financial Studies,* 11(1), 43.

Fleming, J, B Ostdiek and R Whaley (1996). Predicting stock market volatility: A new measure. *Journal of Futures Markets,* 15, 265–302.

Floracki s, C (2008). Agency costs and corporate governance mechanisms: Evidence for UK firms. *International Journal of Managerial Finance*, 4(1), 37–59.

Francis, JR and J Krishnan (1999). Accounting accruals and auditor reporting conservatism. *Contemporary Accounting Research*, 16(1), 135–165.

Francis, JR, K Reichelt, and D Wang (2005). The pricing of national and city-specific reputations for industry expertise in the US audit market. *The Accounting Review*, 80(1), 113–136.

Frankel, JA and D Romer (June 1999). Does trade cause growth. *The American Economic Review*, 89(3), 379–399.

Fremault-Vila, A and G Sandmann (1995). Floor Trading Versus Electronic Screen Trading: An Empirical Analysis of Market Liquidity and Information Transmission in the Nikkei Stock Index Futures Markets, Document 218, London School of Economics.

French, AN, TJ Schugge and WP Kustas (2000). Discrimination of senescent vegetation using thermal emissivity contrast. *Remote Sensing of Environment*, 74, 249–254.

Frino, A, T McInish and M Toner (1998). The liquidity of automated exchanges: New evidence from German bund futures. *Journal of International Financial Markets, Institutions & Money*, 8, 225–241.

Froot, K and A Perold (1995). New trading practices and short-run market efficiency. *Journal of Futures Markets*, 15, 731–765.

Gaffard, J-L (1997). *Croissance et fluctuations économiques*, p. 386, Paris: Montchrestien.

Garbe, CS *et al.* (2002). Thermographic measurements on plant leafs. *Thermosense XXIV*, Orlando, Florida,1–5 Avril 2002.

Gardner, BR *et al.* (1981). Relationship between crop temperature ans the physiological and phenological development of differentially irrigated corn. *Agronomy Journal*, 73, 743–747.

Gendron, Y and J Bédard (2006). On the constitution of audit committee effectiveness. *Accounting, Organizations and Society*, 31(3), 211–239.

Geneviève Morency (2012). La décroissance économique est-elle pertinente? *Horizons économiques*, 2(1), 3.

Gerschenkron, A (1962). *Economic Backwardness in Historical Perspective: A Book of Essays*, p. 456. Cambridge: Belknap Press of Harvard University Press.

Gillet, R and A Minguet (1995). *Micro-structure et rénovation des marchés financiers en Europe*. Paris: PUF.

Goldsmith RW (1969). *Financial Structure and Development.* New Haven: Yale University Press.

Goodhart, C and M O'Hara (1997). High frequency data in financial markets: Issues and applications. *Journal of Empirical Finance,* 4, 73–114.

Gouvernement du Canada (1991). *L'État de l'environnement au Canada.* Altona: DW Friesen & Sons Ltd.

Green, DL (1994). Canadian audit committees and their contribution to corporate governance. *Journal of International Accounting, Auditing and Taxation,* 3(2), 135–151.

Greenwood, J and B Jovanovic (1990). Financial development, growth, and the distribution of income. *Journal of Political Economy,* 98, 1076–1107.

Gregg, P, S Machin and S Szymanski (1993). The disappearing relationship between directors' pay and corporate performance. *British Journal of Industrial Relations,* 31(1), 1–9.

Greif, A (October 1994). Cultural beliefs and the organization of society: A historical and theoretical reflection on collectivist and individuallist societies. *Journal of Political Economy,* 102(5), 912–950.

Greif, A (2006). *Institutions and the Path to the Modern Economy: Lessons from Medieval Trade.* New York: Cambridge University Press.

Griffiths, M *et al.* (1998). Information flows and open outcry: Evidence of imitation trading. *Journal of International Financial Markets, Institutions & Money,* 8, 101–116.

Grime, JP (1989). Whole-plant responses to stress in natural and agricultural systems. In *Plants Under Stress,* HG Jones, TJ Flowers and MB Jones (eds.), pp. 31–46. New York: Cambridge University Press.

Grossman, G and E Helpman (1991). *Innovation and Growth in the Global Economy,* p. 359. Cambridge: MIT Press.

Grossman, SJ and MH Miller (1986). Liquidity and market structure, *The Journal of Finance,* 43, 617–633.

Groupe Céréaliers de France, I (1999). Dossier: Agriculture de précision: Cap sur le XXI ième siècle. 2002.

Grünbichler, A, F Longstaff and E Schwartz (1994). Electronic screen trading and the transmission of information: An empirical examination. *Journal of Financial Intermediation,* 3, 166–187.

Guellec, D and P Ralle (1995). *Les nouvelles théories de la croissance,* p. 123. Paris: Coll. Repères, La découverte.

Guest, PM (2009). The impact of board size on firm performance: Evidence from the UK. *The European Journal of Finance,* 15(4), 385–404.

Gugler, K and BB Yurtoglu (2003). Average q, marginal q, and the relation between ownership and performance. *Economics Letters,* 78(3), 379–384.

Gurbuz, AO and A Aybars (2010). The impact of foreign ownership on firm performance, evidence from an emerging market: Turkey. *American Journal of Economics and Business Administration,* 2(4), 350–359.

Guyot, G (1989). *Signatures spectrales des surfaces naturelles.* Caen: Paradigme.

Gwilym, O, A Clare and S Thomas (1998). Price clustering and bid-ask spreads in international bond futures. *Journal of International Financial Markets, Institutions & Money,* 8, 377–391.

Haboudane, D *et al.* (2002). Integrated narrow-band vegetation indices for prediction of crop chlorophyll content for application to precision agriculture. *Remote Sensing of Environment,* 81, 416–426.

Hamon, J (1995). Marchés d'actions, Economica, Paris. FINÉCO, vol. 9, No 1, 1er semestre 1999 65

Han, L, J Kling and C Sell (1999). Foreign exchange futures volatility: Day-of-the-week, intraday, and maturity patterns in the presence of macroeconomic announcements. *Journal of Futures Markets,* 19, 665–693.

Hardouvelis, G and D Kim (1996). Price volatility and futures margins. *Journal of Futures Markets,* 16, 81–111.

Harris, PM (1992). *The potato crop — The Scientific Basis for Improvement.* London: Chapman et Hall.

Harvey, N (1996). Les marchés des contrats à terme sur acceptations bancaires canadiennes, Revue de la Banque du Canada (Automne), 19–36.

Hausman, JA (1978). Specification tests in econometrics. *Econometrica: Journal of the Econometric Society,* 46, 1251–1271.

Hay, D, W Knechel and H Ling (2008). Evidence on the impact of internal control and corporate governance on audit fees. *International Journal of Auditing,* 12(1), 9–24.

Heller, R, R Esnault and C Lance (1993). Physiologie végétale. Paris: Masson.

Heller, R, R Esnault and C Lance (1998). Physiologie végétale. Paris: Dunod.

Henry, D (2010). Agency costs, ownership structure and corporate governance compliance: A private contracting perspective. *Pacific-Basin Finance Journal,* 18(1), 24–46.

Herbst, A and E Maberly (1992). The informational role of end-of-the-day returns in stock index futures. *Journal of Futures Markets,* 12, 595–601.

Iihara, Y, K Kato and T Tokunaga (1996). Intraday return dynamics between the cash and the futures markets in Japan. *Journal of Futures Markets,* 16, 147–162.

Jones, HG, TJ Flowers and MB Jones (1989). *Plants under Stress.* Cambridge: Cambridge University Press.

Kawaller, I.G., Koch, P.D. et T.W. Koch, 1987, The temporal price relationship between S&P 500 futures and the S&P 500 index. *The Journal of Finance,* 42, 1309–1329.

Kempf, A and O Korn (1996). Trading System and Market Integration, Compte-rendu du congrès: Organisation et qualité des marchés boursiers, Paris.

Kim, M, A Szakmary and T Schwartz (1999). Trading costs and price discovery across stock index futures and cash markets. *Journal of Futures Markets,* 19, 475–498.

King, RG and R Levine (1993a). Finance and growth: Schumpeter might be right. *The Quarterly Journal of Economics,* 108, 717–738.

King RG and R Levine (1993c). Finance intermediation and economic development. In *Financial Intermediation in the Construction of Europe,* C Mayer and X Vives (eds.), pp. 156–189. London: Centre for Economic Policy Research.

Kogagil, A and Y Shachmurove (1998). Return-volume dynamics in future markets. *Journal of Futures Markets,* 18, 399–426.

Kolbe, H and S Stephan-Beckmann (1997a). Development, growth and chemical composition of the potato crop (solanum tuberosum) 1. leaf and stem. *Potato Research,* 40, 111–129.

Kolbe, H and S Stephan-Beckmann (1997b). Development, growth and chemical composition of the potato crop (*solanum tuberosum*). 2. Tuber and plant. *Potato Research,* 40, 135–153.

Krishnan, J and PC Schauer (2000). The differentiation of quality among auditors: Evidence from the not-for-profit sector. *Auditing: A Journal of Practice & Theory,* 19(2), 9–25.

Kuserk, GJ and PR Locke (1993). Scalper behavior in futures markets: An empirical examination. *Journal of Futures Markets,* 13, 409–431.

Kuserk, GJ and PR Locke (1996). Market making with price limits. *Journal of Future Markets,* 16, 677–696.

Kydland F and P Edward (1982). Time to build and aggregate fluctuations. *Econometrica,* 50, 1345–1371.

La Porta, R *et al.* (1998). Law and Finance, *Journal of Political Economy,* 106, 1113–1155.

Lam, T-Y and S-K Lee (2012). Family ownership, board committees and firm performance: evidence from Hong Kong. *Corporate Governance*, 12(3), 353–366.

Langkilde, N (11–15 July 1999). *Practical Experiences with Precision Agriculture. Precision Agriculture '99, Odense Congress Centre.* Danemark: Scheffield Academic Press.

Larcker, DF, SA Richardson and I Tuna (2007). Corporate governance, accounting outcomes, and organizational performance. *The Accounting Review*, 82(4), 963–1008.

LEAD (2001). Boîte à outils Élevage-Environnement, Organisme des Nations Unies pour l'Alimentation et l'Agriculture. 2002.

Leblon, B *et al.* (2001). *Use of geomatics in precision agriculture. Planète Virtuelle 2001.* Fredericton: Nouveau-Brunswick.

Lee, C, B Mucklow and M Ready (1993). Spreads, depths and the impact of earnings information: An intraday analysis. *Review of Financial Studies*, 6, 345–374.

Lee, S (2008). Ownership structure and financial performance: Evidence from panel data of South Korea: Working Paper, University of Utah, Department of Economics.

Leng, A (2004). The impact of corporate governance practices on firms' financial performance: Evidence from Malaysian companies. *Asean Economic Bulletin*, 21(3), 308–318.

Leng, H (1996). Announcement versus nonannouncement: A study of intraday transaction price paths of Deutsche Mark and Japanese Yen futures. *Journal of Futures Markets*, 16, 829–857.

Lennox, C (1999). Are large auditors more accurate than small auditors? *Accounting and Business Research*, 29(3), 217–227.

Leonard, JS (1990). Executive pay and firm performance. Industrial and Labor Relations Review, 43(3), 13–29.

Lequeux, P and P Dugue (1998). A statistical view of the liffe bund future. *Quarterly Review (Liffe)*, 17–20.

Levine, R (1997). Financial Development and economic Growth: Views and Agenda. *Journal of Economic Litterature*, 35, 688–729.

Levine, R (2002). Bank-based or market-based financial systems: Which is better? *Journal of Financial Intermediation*, 11, 398–428.

Levine, R (2005). Finance and growth: Theory and evidence. In *Handbook of Economic Growth*, P Aghion and S Durlauf (eds.), pp. 866–934. Amsterdam: North-Holland.

Levine, R and S Zervos (1998a). Stock markets, banks, and economic growth. *American Economic Review*, 88, 537–558.

Lewellen, W *et al.* (1992). Executive compensation and the performance of the firm. *Managerial and Decision Economics*, 13(1), 65–74.

Li, PH (1985). *Potato Physiology*. Orlando: Academic Press.

Li, Z and L Moreau (1996a). A new approach for remote sensing of canopy-absorbed photosynthetically active radiation. 1: Total surface absorption. *Remote Sensing of Environment*, 55(3), 175–191.

Li, Z and L Moreau (1996b). A new approach for remote sensing of canopy-absorbed photosynthetically active radiation. 2: Proportion of canopy absorption. *Remote Sensing of Environment*, 55(3), 192–204.

Li, Z-L *et al.* (1999). Evaluation of six methods for extracting relative emissivity spectra from thermal infrared images. *Remote Sensing of Environement*, 69(3), 197–214.

Lichtenthaler, HK *et al.* (1998). Plant stress detection by reflectance and fluorescence. *Annals of the New-York Academy of Sciences*, 851, 271–285.

LI-COR inc. (1988). *LI-3000A Portable Area Meter LI-3050A Transparent BElt Conveyer Instruction Manual.* Lincoln: LI-COR inc.

Liption, M and J Lorsch (1992). A modest proposal for improved corporate governance, A. *The Business Lawyer*, 48(1), 59–77.

Locke, PR and PC Venkatesh (1997). Futures Market Transaction Costs. *Journal of Futures Markets*, 17, 229–245.

Lucas, RE (1988). On the mechanics of economic development. *Journal of Monetary Economics*, 22, 3–42.

Ma, C, R Peterson and S Sears (1992). Trading noise, adverse selection and in- traday bid-ask spreads in futures markets, *Journal of Futures Markets*, 12, 519–538.

Mannaï, S (1995). *De la microstructure en général et de la liquidité en particulier*, Paris: Economica.

MAPAQ (1998). Engagements des décideurs du forum sur l'agriculture et l'agroalimentaire québécois 5 et 6 mars 1998 St-Hyacinthe, Gouvernement du Québec. 2002.

MAPAQ (2000). Forum sur la croissance de l'agriculture et de l'agroalimentaire québécois, Rendez-vous des décideurs- Conclusions su Rendez-vous, le 25 mars 1999 à Québec, Gouvernement du Québec. 2002.

MAPAQ (2001a). Bonnes pratiques agroenvironnementales pour votre entreprise agricole, MAPAQ (Ministère de l'Agriculture, des Pêcheries et de l'Alimentation du Québec).

MAPAQ (2001b). Signature d'une entente sur l'écoconditionnalité. Les producteurs de porcs du Québec accélèrent leur virage vert, Cabinet du ministre Maxime Arseneau.

MAPAQ and A Canada (1997). Rationalisation de l'engrais azoté dans la culture de la pomme de terre par l'optimisation du fractionnemnt de l'azote et de l'utilisation du dris: 91.

Massimb, M and B Phelps (1994). Electronic trading, market structure and liquidity. *Financial Analysts Journal (Janvier-Février)*, 50, 39–50.

Mehran, H (1995). Executive compensation structure, ownership, and firm performance. *Journal of Financial Economics*, 38(2), 163–184.

Merton, RC (1995). A Functional Perspective of Financial Intermediation. *Financial Management*, 24, 23–41.

Minolta Co. Ltd (1989). Chlorophyll meter SPAD-502 Instruction manual.

Moran, MS *et al.* (1994). Estimating crop water deficit using the relation between surface-air temperature and spectral vegatation index. *Remote sensing of environment*, 49(3), 246–263.

Nelson, RR (1995). Recent evolutionary theorizing about economic change. *Journal of Economic Literature*, 33, 48–90.

Nelson, RR (1996). *The Sources of Economic Growth.* Cambridge: Harvard University Press.

Nelson, RR and S Winter (1982). *An Evolutionary Theory of Economic Change.* London: The Belknap Press of Harvard University.

Nobel, PS (1991). *Physicochemical and Environmental Plant Physiology.* San Diego: Academic Press.

O'Connor, S (1993). L'évolution des marchés canadiens des produits financiers dérivés. Revue de la Banque du Canada (Automne), 53–64.

O'Hara, M (1995). *Market Microstructure Theory.* New York: Basil Blackwell.

OCDE (2001a). *Améliorer les performances environnementales de l'agriculture: choix de mesures et approches par le marché.* Paris: OCDE.

OCDE (2001b). *Indicateurs environnementaux pour l'agriculture — Méthodes et résultats.* Paris: OCDE.

Oesch, D (2001). L'inégalité, frein à la croissance? L'effet de l'inégalité des revenus sur les taux de croissance de dix pays de l'Europe de l'Ouest, *dans Swiss Political Science Review*, 7(2), 27–48.

Office de la langue française du Québec (2002). Le grand dictionnaire terminologique, Gouvernement du Québec. 2002.

Orcutt, DM and ET Nilsen (2000). *The Physiology of Plants Under Stress.* New York: John Wiley and Sons.

Parent, L-É (1998). Fertilisation des agroécosystèmes, guide pédagogique du cours SLS-64885, Département des sols et de génie agroalimentaire de Université Laval. Québec, Service des ressources pédagogiques de l'Université Laval.

Pavia, DL, GM Lampman and GS Kriz (1996). Introduction to spectroscopy. Orlando: Harcourt Brace College.

Peng, S *et al.* (1993). Adjustment for specific leaf weight improves chlorophyll meter's estimate of rice leaf nitrogen concentration. *Agronomy Journal*, 85(5). 987–990.

Perrakis, S and N Khoury 1998, Asymmetric information in commodity futures markets: Theory and empirical evidence. *Journal of Futures Markets*, 18, 803–825.

Phan, D-L (1982). *Economie de la croissance*, p. 292. Paris: Economica.

Pirrong, C (1996). Market liquidity and depth on computerized and outcry trading systems: A comparison of DTB and Liffe bund contracts. *Journal of Futures Markets*, 16, 519–543.

Plant, RE (2001). Site-specific management: The application of information technology to crop production. *Computers and Electronics in Agriculture*, 30, 9–29.

Quine, B (2001). *WebGen: Spectroscopic Absorption Calculator.* University of Toronto. 2002.

Radtke, W and W Rieckmann (1991). *Maladies et ravageurs de la pomme de terre.* Gelsenkirchen-Buer: Verlag Th. Mann.

Rajan, R and L Zingales (1998). Financial dependence and growth. *American Economic Review*, 88, 559–586.

Raun, WR and GV Johnson (1999). Improving nitrogen use efficiency for cereal production. *Agronomy Journal*, 91, 357–363.

Ray, JD and TR Sinclair (1998). The effect of pot size on growth and transpiration of maize and soybean during water deficit stress. *Journal of Experimental Botany*, 49(325), 1381–1386.

Read, JJ *et al.* (2002). Narrow-waveband reflectance ratios for remote estimation of nitrogen status in cotton. *Journal of Environmental Quality*, 31, 1442–1452.

Régie des Assurances agricoles du Québec (1997). Le mesurage des champs par ordinateurs. Nouvelle méthode, Gouvernement du Québec. 2002.

Richards, JA and X Jia (1999). *Remote Sensing Digital Image Analysis- An introduction.* Berlin: Springer.

Robert, PC (1999). *Precision Agriculture: Research needs and Status in the USA. Precision Agriculture '99, Odense Congress Centre.* Danemark, 11-15 juillet 1999, Scheffield Academic Press.

Robert, PC, RH Rust and WE Larson (1994). Preface in Site-specific management for agricultural systems. In *Site-Specific Management for Agricultural Systems: Second International Conference.* Minneapolis, Minessota 27–30 mars 1994, Soil Science Society of America.

Roll, R (1984). A simple implicit measure of the effective bid-ask spread in an efficient market. *The Journal of Finance,* 39, 1127–1139.

Rouse, JW *et al.* (1973). Monitoring vegetation systems in the great plains with ERTS. In *Third Earth Resources Technology Satellite-1 Symposium.* Goddard Space Flight Center, NASA.

Saint-Paul, G (1992). Technological choice, financial markets and economic development. *European Economic Review,* 36, 763–781.

Sanders, D, SH Irwin and R Leuthold (1997). Noise Traders, Market Sentiment, and Futures Price Behavior, Working paper, Ohio State University.

SAS Institute Inc. (1999). *SAS OnLineDoc V8.* Cary: Statistical Analysis System Institute.

Schepers, JS *et al.* (1992). Comparison of corn leaf nitrogen concentration and chlorophyll meter readings. *Communications in Soil Science and Plant Analysis,* 23(17–20), 2173–2187.

Schepers, JS *et al.* (1996). Transmittance and reflectance measurements of corn leaves from plant with different nitrogen and water supply. *Journal of Plant Physiology,* 148, 523–529.

Schmugge, TJ and WP Kustas (1999). Radiometry at infrared wavelengths for agricultural applications. *Agronomie,* 19(2), 83–96.

Schmugge, T *et al.* (2002). Temperature and emissivity separation from multispectral thermal infrared observations. *Remote Sensing of Environment,* 79, 189–198.

Schröder, JJ *et al.* (2000). Does the crop or the soil indicate how to save nitrogen in maize production? Reviewing the state of the art. *Field Crops Research,* 66, 151–164.

Schumpeter, J (1912). *Theorie der Wirtschaftlichen Entwicklung* [*The Theory of Economic Development*], Leipzig: Dunker & Humblot, 1912; translated by Redvers Opie, Cambridge: Harvard University Press, 1934.

Shaw, ES (1973). *Financial Deepening in Economic Development,* New York: Oxford University Press.

Shyy, G and JH Lee (1995). Price transmission and information asymmetry in bund futures markets: Liffe vs. DTB. *Journal of Futures Markets*, 15, 87–99.

Shyy, G, V Vijayraghavan and B Scott-Quinn (1996). A further investigation of the lead-lag relationship between the cash market and stock index futures market with the use of bid/ask quotes: The case of France. *Journal of Futures Markets*, 16, 405–420.

Silber, WL (1984). Marketmaker behavior in an auction market: An analysis of scalpers. *The Journal of Finance*, 39, 937–953.

Silverberg G, and M Yildizoglu (1992). An Evolutionary Interpretation of the Aghion & Howitt (1992) Model.

Simon, Y (1998). *Marchés à terme de taux d'intérêt*. Paris: Economica.

Sirri, ER and P Tufano (1995). The economic of pooling. In *The Global Financial System: A functional Appraoch*, DB Crane *et al.* (eds.), pp. 81–128. Boston: Harvard Business School Press.

Smeal, D and H Zhang (1994). Chlorophyll meter evaluation for nitrogen management in corn. *Communications in Soil Science and Plant Analysis*, 25(9–10), 1495–1503.

Smith, A (1776). *An Inquiry into the Nature and Causes of the Wealth of Nations*. London: W. Stahan & T. Cadell.

Smith, T and R Whaley (1994). Estimating the effective bid-ask spreads from time and sales data. *Journal of Futures Markets*, 14, 437–455.

Stafford, JV (2000). Implementing precision agriculture in the 21st century. *Journal of Agricultural Engineering Research*, 76(3), 267–275.

Statistique Canada (2001). Le Canada en statistiques, CANSIM II, tableaux 379-0019 et 379-0022 et produit no 15-001-XIF au catalogue, Statistique Canada. 2002.

Statistiques Canada (2002). Production canadienne de pommes de terre. 2002.

Stephan, J and R Whaley (1990). Intraday price change and trading volume relations in stock & stock option markets. *The Journal of Finance*, 45, 191–220.

Stiglitz, J and A Weiss (June 1981). Credit rationing in markets with imperfect information. *American Economic Review*, 71(3), 393–410.

Stiglitz, J and A Weiss (1983). Incentive effects of terminations: Applications to credit and labor markets. *American Economic Review*, 73(5), 912–927.

Stombaugh, TS and S Shearer (2000). Equipment technologies for precision agriculture. *Journal of Soil and Water Conservation*, 55(1), 6–11.

St-Pierre, J (2002). 80 ans d'histoire, l'histoire de la Coopérative fédérée, Coopérative fédérée de Québec. 2002.

Stulz, RM (2001). Does financial structure matter for economic growth? A corporate finance perspective. In *Financial Structure and Economic Growth: A Cross-Country Comparison of Banks, Markets, and Development*, A Demirg-Kunt and R Levine (eds.), pp. 143–188. Cambridge: MIT Press.

Tadesse, S (2002). Financial architecture and economic performance: International evidence. *Journal of Financial Intermediation*, 11, 429–454.

Tellefsen, A *et al.* (1999). The matching game. *Futures Industry* (Avril-Mai), 9–15.

Thomas, JR and HW Gausmann (1977). Leaf reflectance vs. leaf chlorophyll and carotenoid concentration for eight crops. *Agronomy Journal*, 69, 799–802.

Thompson, S and ML Waller (1988). Determinants of liquidity costs in commodity futures markets. *Review of Futures Markets*, 7, 110–126.

Thomsen, S and T Pedersen (2000). Ownership structure and economic performance in the largest European companies. *Strategic Management Journal*, 21(6), 689–705.

Tsang, R (1999). Cotation à la criée et cotation électronique dans les bourses de contrats à terme. Revue de la Banque du Canada (Printemps), 21–37.

Tse, Y (1998). International linkages in Euromark futures markets: Information transmission and market integration. *Journal of Futures Markets*, 18, 129–149.

Tse, Y (1999a). Market microstructure of FT-SE 100 index futures: An intraday empirical analysis. *Journal of Futures Markets*, 19, 31–58.

Tse, Y (1999b). Price discovery and volatility spillovers in the DJIA index and futures markets. *Journal of Futures Markets*, 19, 911–930.

Uadiale, OM (2010). The impact of board structure on corporate financial performance in Nigeria. *International Journal of Business and Management*, 5(10), 155–166.

Ulibarri, C (1998). Is after-hours trading informative? *Journal of Futures Markets*, 18, 563–579.

UPA (2002). Le monde de l'agriculture, une industrie vitale. 2002.

Viau, AA (23–24 March 2000a). Agriculture de précision et géomatique agricole: vers une définition. In *1er colloque sur la géomatique agricole et l'agriculture de précision*. St-Hyacinthe.

Viau, AA (23–24 March 2000b). La géomatique et la collecte de données en agriculture. In *1er colloque sur la géomatique agricole et l'agriculture de précision*, St-Hyacinthe.

Vogt, JV *et al.* (2000). Drought monitoring from space. In *Drought and drought mitigation in Europe*. JV Vogt *et al.* (eds.), Vol. 14, pp. 167–183. Kluwer Academic Publishers.

Wang, G *et al.* (1994). An intraday analysis of bid-ask spreads and price volatility in the S&P 500 index futures market. *Journal of Futures Markets*, 4, 837–859.

Wang, G, J Yau and T Baptiste (1997). Trading volume and transaction costs in futures markets. *Journal of Futures Markets*, 17, 757–780.

Watt, D (1997). Canadian Short-Term Interest Rates and the BAX Futures Market, Document 97-18, Banque du Canada.

Webb, R and D Smith (1994). The effect of market opening and closing on the volatility of Eurodollar futures prices. *Journal of Futures Markets*, 14, 51–78.

Weber, J and M Willenborg (2003). Do expert informational intermediaries add value? Evidence from auditors in microcap initial public offerings. *Journal of Accounting Research*, 41(4), 681–720.

Wei, Z, F Xie, and S Zhang (2005). Ownership structure and firm value in China's privatized firms: 1991–2001. *The Journal of Financial and Quantitative Analysis*, 40(1), 87–108.

Westcott, MP and JM Wraith (1995). Correlation of leaf chlorophyll readings and stem nitrate concentrations in peppermint. *Communications in Soil Science and Plant Analysis*, 26(9–10), 1481–1490.

Wiley, M and R Daigler (1998). Volume relationships among types of traders in the financial futures markets. *Journal of Futures Markets*, 18, 91–113.

Willenborg, M (1999). Empirical analysis of the economic demand for auditing in the initial public offerings market. *Journal of Accounting Research*, 37(1), 225–238.

Wu, D-M (1973). Alternative tests of independence between stochastic regressors and disturbances. *Econometrica: Journal of the Econometric Society*, 41, 733–750.

Zarco-Tejada, PJ *et al.* (2002). Vegetation stress detection through Chlorophyll a+b estimation and fluorescence effects on hyperspectral imagery. *Journal of Environmental Quality*, 31, 1433–1441.

Printed in the United States
By Bookmasters